Strategic
Alliances

Publisher's Note: Memo to the CEO

Authored by leading experts and examining issues of special urgency, the books in the Memo to the CEO series are tailored for today's time-starved executives. Concise, focused, and solutions-oriented, each book explores a critical management challenge and offers authoritative counsel, provocative points of view, and practical insight.

Also available:

Strategic Alliances

Three Ways to Make Them Work

Steve Steinhilber

Harvard Business Press

Boston, Massachusetts

No part of this publication may be reproduced, stored in or introduced into a retrieval system, or transmitted, in any form, or by any means (electronic, mechanical, photocopying, recording, or otherwise), without the prior permission of the publisher. Requests for permission should be directed to permissions@hbsp.harvard.edu, or mailed to Permissions, Harvard Business School Publishing, 60 Harvard Way, Boston, Massachusetts 02163.

Library of Congress Cataloging-in-Publication Data
Steinhilber, Steve.
   Strategic alliances : three ways to make them work / Steve Steinhilber.
       p.   cm.
   ISBN 978-1-4221-2588-5
   1. Strategic alliances (Business) I. Title.
   HD69.S8S727 2008
   658'.046—dc22

                                                        2008027504

The paper used in this publication meets the requirements of the American National Standard for Permanence of Paper for Publications and Documents in Libraries and Archives Z39.48-1992

Contents

Why Ally?

If you're reading this book, most likely you've formed strategic alliances with other companies or are considering starting one in the future. You may have already had some success, but just as likely, you may also see the wreckage of failed alliances all around you.

More than two thousand strategic alliances are launched worldwide each year, and these partnerships are growing at 15 percent annually.[1] Yet despite all the growth and headlines, slightly more than half of all strategic partnerships fail. More than one-third of companies that take part in alliances struggle with them. Only 9 percent consistently build alliances well.[2]

This performance begs three questions: What is a strategic alliance? Why should companies continue to focus resources on creating and managing these relationships considering the poor success rate? After all, isn't it always easier to do something yourself? As someone with the responsibility for overall shareholder return, you must certainly ask these questions.

You want to know whether an investment in a strategic alliance stacks up against your company's other investment opportunities.

But more important, I believe there's a right, and a wrong, way to build alliances. Do them right, and you will achieve significantly higher and more consistent shareholder returns. Your company will grow faster and more profitably when you leverage alliances instead of going it alone.

Let's start by defining the term *strategic alliance*. While there are many viewpoints, simply put, it is a relationship between one or more organizations that—through the combination of resources—can create significant and sustainable value for everyone involved. Over the years we at Cisco have evolved five basic criteria to identify and characterize such relationships:

- **Significant business impact with sustainable value:** *Significant* is always defined relative to the stakeholders, and *sustainable* means generating acceptable profit margins over a multiyear period.

- **Broad and deep initiatives:** *Broad* to me means "several," and *deep* signals "significant" initiatives within the alliance that cut across the value chains of both companies.

- **Strong organizational commitment:** Such commitment must flow from the CEO down and be marked by clear ownership at senior levels and by accountable alliance management teams.

- **Substantial investment by both companies:** Investment can be people, capital, intellectual property, or all three.

- **Strategic alignment and fit:** The companies' strategies in the targeted space must be well aligned. Although their cultures may be different, the companies must be able to establish an environment of trust.

I believe there are three reasons why alliances are a must-do investment for any company competing in the global marketplace:

- **Product life cycles:** Product life cycles are becoming shorter and shorter. This requires companies to quickly achieve global share and significant volumes to compete and generate adequate return on investment. Few companies have the necessary ability and capital in all segments of their value chain to achieve these objectives operating solo.

- **Anytime/anywhere communication:** Enhanced communication technologies and cheap bandwidth are enabling services and capabilities to be delivered from anywhere in the world. That puts severe pressure on companies as products and processes become commoditized and static value chains become disaggregated. You must focus on what you do well while relying on partners to complete the pieces of the value chain needed for your business to grow profitably.

- **Customer expectations:** Both businesses and consumers expect and demand more integrated solutions to solve their needs, pushing companies to work together to create differentiated offerings. No company has enough expertise or capital to go it alone. Having the skills to create, modify, and sustain these integrated solutions will be key for any company in the evolving global environment.

You can see the advantages of partnering across a wide range of industries. To address the problem of higher drug development costs and long approval lead times, pharmaceutical companies like Eli Lilly are increasingly pursuing relationships with networks of small companies to develop and market new drugs. In the high-tech field, Sony and Ericsson have combined their mobile-handset units in a joint venture to leverage both companies' R&D and distribution competencies to take on larger competitors, like Nokia and Motorola. In transportation, three major airline alliances now account for half of the global passenger market, offering more flights to more locations, better connections, and consolidated frequent-flier programs on a global scale. In the energy business, Chevron and Texaco have a time-tested alliance in the Middle East that produces more than $11 billion in revenues for both companies.[3]

Strategic alliances have been invaluable in helping Cisco grow and move into new markets, ranging from storage switching to wireless LANs to IP telephony. It's also helped us move into key vertical markets and accelerate growth in new regions like Japan, eastern Europe, and India.

We've worked with IBM, for example, to develop multiple solutions integrating the technologies and services from both companies. Examples include supply chain management for manufacturers, branch banking for the financial services community, and IPTV for major telecom service providers. On another front, we worked with HP and Norwegian medical software company Baze Technology to develop a digital hospital infrastructure. Doctors and nurses can now collaborate on patient diagnosis and treatment in real time anywhere on a medical campus with a range of wireless devices. We've also built products for telecom service providers that enable them to provide unified communications to the small- and medium-business marketplace. The list goes on and on. Strategic alliances have helped fuel Cisco's growth. The company wouldn't be where it is today without its partners.

When an Alliance Is *Not* the Answer

When selecting a business strategy, it is important to remember that strategic alliances are just one business tool that, if used at the wrong time, can materially hurt an organization. You must be able to step back and look at your three options. Should you build a capacity yourself, buy it through an acquisition, or strategically partner? You don't have to choose one option. The real power and benefit to your organization often comes when you understand how all three of these strategic options can be used simultaneously to help your company address a new market opportunity.

Alliances do not make sense when your organization has the requisite skills and resources necessary to win a battle on its own in a targeted market space.

Alliances also do not make sense when you need to control a certain technology, skill, or capability to ensure your company's long-term success and profitability. If you have the capability and the market window will stay open, build this technology or skill yourself. If you don't have the capability or the market window won't stay open, if there are reasonably priced targets, and if you have the capital, then an acquisition can be a far better answer than an alliance.

It is critical that your organization make the appropriate trade-offs among these three options early in the strategy-setting process and then execute on them when you've made your decisions. If you think a strategic alliance can be a key component of your strategy, read on.

The Right Way to Think About Alliances

This memo is about how enduring and mutually beneficial global business relationships help you create the leverage you need to compete. It's ultimately about the *right way* to partner.

Building alliances right requires several ingredients: partnerships play an integral part of your company's strategy, you have a repeatable and sustainable process, and you're building both the necessary competencies and reputation for success.

At Cisco, I manage a portfolio of alliances that crosses multiple industry sectors, technologies, and geographies, with a cumulative value of more than $4.5 billion annually in business impact to Cisco and much more than that to our alliance partners. Strategic alliances are woven into the very fabric of our company and the way we see ourselves in the world— from Chairman and CEO John Chambers on down. You'll see a similar picture at other alliance-savvy companies, like IBM, Eli Lilly, and Procter & Gamble— partnerships are a central part of their core strategy.

If alliances are not viewed as an integral part of *your* strategy, then you're working with both hands tied behind your back. You might have a few short-term successes, but long term, make no mistake: *you will probably fail.*

Let's assume that you have a strategy in which alliances do make sense for your company at one or more levels of your value chain. If that's the case, you need to construct and manage each alliance as a business. Your job is to bring the right framework, the right organization, and the right relationships together and to move the project forward. Your approach needs to look at the big picture rather than short-term payoffs. "Winning" and beating the other company in negotiations may doom the relationship from the beginning. One of the biggest mistakes you can make is thinking that alliances are all about hammering out an airtight deal structure, negotiating hard, and planning for every eventuality. We had one partner whose CEO said he measured a partnership's success "in the number of POs [purchase orders] that get written"—in other words, how much business *his company* generated from *us*. That company is no longer a partner.

The *right way* to think about partnering revolves around negotiating win-win agreements and growing the market for everyone. If you are spending your time in the discussions worried about dividing a pie that is not growing, you are probably not looking through the right lens. Think in terms of building incremental value and creating a bigger pie, not just getting the fattest slice.

In short, we've found that successful alliances require three essential building blocks:

- **The right framework:** Start with a strategy, not a partner. Clearly identify how and where an alliance will help you achieve your business goals, who might be potential partners, and the short- and long-term wins for the companies involved. Then you need an efficient, repeatable model based on a set of best practices and a coherent strategy. Following an alliance playbook can actually reduce risk, create a platform for making decisions, minimize conflicts (or help resolve them), and dramatically increase returns. And having a truly repeatable process can cut the failure rate by more than half.

- **The right organization:** Alliance managers are the driving force of your strategy. Sadly, many companies pick the wrong types of people to staff the organization and then systematically fail to invest adequate resources in their employees' training and development. Alliance managers are a rare breed: they must be equal parts diplomat, salesperson, strategist, and orchestra conductor, and you need to clearly spell out the requirements for their success. Then you must constantly hone their skills.

- **The right relationships:** At the end of the day, partnerships are relationships—between alliance managers on each team, between the teams and their executive sponsors, and between the alliance manager and key internal contacts in the business units, sales channels, business development staff, and so on. Strong relationships are the glue that holds all these people together. The biggest reason many alliances fail revolves around trust. Trust between two companies can take years to build but can be destroyed in only a few minutes with the wrong move. It's important to understand that you must manage relationships with the right blend of both science *and* art: with first-rate people skills and a systematic process for strengthening connections.

If you think that building an alliance is all about doing the deal and winning at all costs, you're in for a rude surprise. You have to analyze your alliance strategy through a new lens, starting with those three factors. You have to think differently.

This memo is not a tell-all book with every answer. I've focused on the essential parts of building and managing a strategic alliance portfolio and program while providing key tips that will help you accelerate your efforts. Even if you're already partnering with other companies, this book will help you clarify your thinking and strategy and avoid some of the biggest pitfalls.

As a CEO, you have many decisions to make on how to spend your shareholders' capital and your executive team's time. Over the next several sections, I hope you will see that investing in strategic alliances is good business for the following reasons:

- **Part of your strategic toolbox:** Alliances are an essential tool that enables you to attack new market opportunities as part of your build-buy-partner decision-making process. Having the ability to use these tools independently or collectively significantly increases your chances of winning new or adjacent markets.

- **Responding more rapidly to changing markets:** In a world where information and product velocity are accelerating and customer needs continue to change, no one company can do it all. You just can't hit all market windows and meet all market requirements alone. Meeting global marketplace requirements with varying market timing often means huge investments. Not meeting these global market needs in many industries may mean you are ceding the high ground to a more powerful competitor in your upcoming strategic battle. Alliances can help you go global—hitting critical market windows and sharing the capital risk.

- **Core versus context focus:** Trying to do it all in a vertically integrated model is becoming harder and harder in most global industries. It's critical to define what is core to your business (that is, essential to how you maintain value) and what is context (that is, activities that support core functions). Geoffrey Moore makes this point in his book *Living on the Fault Line*. Alliances can help you focus on what you do best and what is core to the long-term health of your company. You'll be in a better position to leverage other resources in those activities that are contextual but still important to your business.

- **Required strategic investment:** Investing in a strategic alliance capability should be managed like any other strategic investment you make. Leveraging the true value an alliance can bring to your company requires fully committing your capital and senior management time to make it successful, putting the right metrics in place, and ensuring that you are getting the return you deserve compared to your other alternatives.

The rewards for managing and nourishing relationships are huge. One of our partners was approached by a competitor to leave its deal with Cisco in return for a promise of $1 billion in future revenues. But because we'd build such a strong relationship, that partner chose to stick with us. Its relationship with Cisco has reaped billions of dollars in revenue over the past several years.

That's what this book is about: building long-term relationships and alliances that will help your company grow and prosper.

Using the Right Framework

As John Wooden, a Hall of Fame college basketball player and coach, once said, "Failure to plan is a plan for failure." And likewise, without strong initial plans your alliances will drift aimlessly, reacting to every change that comes along. About half of all alliances break up on the rocks, mainly because of a lack of direction.

In the real world of business, the price of such failure is high. A Harvard Business School/Accenture study found that the fifteen most successful alliances added $72 billion in shareholder value over two years but that the same number of bad alliances *cost* companies $43 billion.[4]

Partnerships fail because they lack an approach to guide both sides as they work together. The number of ad hoc partnerships never ceases to amaze me. Many seem to be thrown together on a whim with little thought given to a systematic process. Instead, alliances require a process and a governance structure—

that is, a disciplined procedure that guides their formation and offers a clear way to make decisions about managing the partnership once it is under way.

In other words, to make partnerships work, you need the right framework.

This is the game plan that guides your strategy through every step of what we at Cisco call the "strategic alliance life cycle."

Cisco's approach is built around a systematic, repeatable process. We do, however, customize each alliance to be in tune with customers' needs and partners' strengths. With a solid alliance framework in place, you can reduce risk, hold stakeholders accountable, set clear expectations, create a platform for decision making, and improve the overall chances of success. You'll be working smarter, rather than simply working harder.

The Life Cycle of Alliances

Just as people undergo certain universal stages of growth and development, successful alliances have a life cycle of their own. They are born, grow, mature, and die in the six stages of the alliance life cycle:

- **Evaluating** a strategy and potential partners

- **Forming** the relationship

- **Incubating** the partnership

- **Operating** the alliance

- **Transitioning** to the next level

- **Retiring** the alliance when it no longer meets mutual goals

At Cisco, we have identified thirty best practices that address the key deliverables across these six stages (see figure 1). They are your checklist and plan to help ensure consistent performance.

Following a plan is not a guarantee for success. You'll also need good leadership skills and favorable operating conditions. However, having a plan dramatically improves the probability that you will achieve your goals.

Evaluating a Strategy and Potential Partners

You can't build a successful relationship if you don't know why you're considering partnering in the first place. So the first stage is simply understanding the problem you need to solve and the potential benefits that any partnership could bring to your customers and your company.

Any potential relationship should align with your corporate strategy. That may sound obvious to sea-

FIGURE 1

Alliance life cycle

Evaluating	Forming	Incubating
• Define strategy	• Examine partnering value proposition	• Structure alliance governance
• Analyze portfolio	• Secure sponsors	• Build model for operations
• Evaluate ecosystem	• Finalize negotiations and agreements	• Plan communications
• Evaluate partner	• Get counsel on intellectual property	• Develop partner engagement model
• Build business case	• Announce alliance	• Finish marketing plan for alliance launch

Operating	Transitioning	Retiring
• Establish executive committees and boards	• Review strategy and value proposition	• Conduct management discussions
• Develop a joint operating plan	• Examine value curves and trends	• Determine exit strategy
• Establish alliance solutions and initiatives	• Update strategy goals	• Build exit plans
• Launch field engagement and marketing	• Confirm joint commitment	• Define activities and timeline
• Create metrics and performance reporting	• Determine future investment	• Create messaging

soned executives, but I've seen too many successful companies simply react to overtures from another firm rather than take a proactive and planned approach. As they learn the hard way, doing the wrong deal can ultimately conflict with a company's overall strategy, introduce destructive competition, and/or pull the firm off course. This does not mean that your company will initiate all of its successful alliances, but a strategic framework should apply to all ideas—whether they come from inside or outside your company.

Leaders need to sit down with product teams and functional groups to understand the opportunities and challenges they are trying to address, determine where gaps exist in the value chain, and drill down into the potential partnering options. It is critically important that you understand the problem and the requirement you are trying to address with a partnering option. That way, you'll understand when it's better to build something in-house, when it's preferable to buy what you need, or when you must ally to grow. As mentioned in section 1, at Cisco we call these options "build," "buy," and "partner."

Start with a clear strategic focus: what are you trying to do—for example, enter a new market or move into a new vertical field?

Based on the definition of the problem, you can move forward with a list of the criteria to use in evaluating potential alliance partners. We use a simple competitive assessment grid to evaluate partners on ten key criteria, including philosophical alignment, aggression and speed, market strength, and knowledge of and commitment to Cisco. We rate the criteria using a red, yellow, and green light system. If enough of the factors combine to form an overall green-light score, we move forward. When we face more than one good partnership option, we agree on the priority order and the approach to each one. In some cases, this could mean moving forward sequentially and, in other cases, in parallel.

Using these criteria, you'll need to identify potential target companies. You probably already know companies that might make good candidates because of market size, industry, product offerings, geography, or other criteria. Use your own criteria and the market intelligence you've gathered to narrow the list to a manageable number of candidates to investigate more thoroughly. Once your due diligence is complete, seek out partners with compatible goals and complementary capabilities. For instance, successful networking technology companies tend to work with system integrators, professional services firms, telecommunications companies, and solutions developers that can complement and enhance their offerings.

Any partnership must satisfy a market need, address customer demand, and meet defined business goals. At Cisco, we often aim to strategically ally with equally big companies that have global reach, products and capabilities we don't already provide, and a footprint in markets that offer the potential for significant business impact—at least $500 million in revenues per year. Occasionally, we may start with a smaller partner who can help us disrupt an existing market or prod some of the larger players to move more quickly, but these are the exception rather than the rule.

If the relationship cuts across multiple functions or groups within our company and has the potential to create a high level of strategic impact, the corporate strategic alliance teams get engaged. If the relationship is only strategic to one particular group, it often can best be managed in a business unit. There is no one model that fits all companies: structure your alliance so that it syncs up with your company's organizational structure and dynamics, and then apply a laserlike focus on the areas that will drive the greatest value.

Once you start to explore a particular relationship, be sure to analyze the partner. Begin building the business case for or against a deal, asking such questions as:

- What customer problem can be addressed more effectively with the relationship?

- Does the partner fill a hole or a need? Companies must need each other and create something neither would have individually.

- Is there portfolio and company alignment? Ask:

  - Is there a depth and breadth of products and services to work with across both companies?

  - Is there too much of an overlap in products or services?

  - What are the strengths and weaknesses of each partner?

  - Can the cultures fit together?

- What is the size of the opportunity? Measure the expected revenue impact, and compare it to the level of investment and overhead of managing the relationship.

Expect to make trade-offs with every alliance. With one alliance we traded improved market access and better competitive positioning for an investment in joint product development. The benefits outweighed some overlap in a few markets. In another deal in a product space where we felt the long-term competitive advantage for Cisco was limited, we used an alliance to follow our strategic plan and licensed our technology in exchange for the partner's support in other areas of our product line. This model enabled the other company to continue to add value and differentiate its core offering while helping make our product the long-term market leader in the space.

When the results of our evaluation are mixed, or internal stakeholders are not in alignment about how to proceed, we use scenario analysis to better understand the trade-offs. Cross-functional teams come together to explore different scenarios and to take on opposing roles. A "red team" can strongly argue for not partnering with the proposed company, and a "green team" focuses on articulating all the reasons why the relationship should move forward. Meanwhile, a "yellow team" attempts to frame the trade-offs.

This vetting of positions ensures that you thoroughly consider the range of views within your company and also lets the group members know that their positions have been heard. Through this process you'll make the best decision while knowing you have a strong base of support across the company.

For many years, Habitat for Humanity, the global not-for-profit organization known for building affordable homes with low-income families, has used a network of alliance partners to accomplish its goals. The alliance program had a simple start: attracting corporate sponsors to help provide building materials, tools, and volunteers to construct homes. It's grown considerably since then to include financial institutions, government organizations, other social service agencies, churches, and many more.

As part of its selection process to choose new alliance partners, Habitat uses a thorough review tool that examines multiple characteristics of a potential fit. The organization's leaders know Habitat's own strengths (including broad community engagement celebrating diversity, high visibility, and opportunity for hands-on involvement with tangible and intrinsic outcomes), and they know its limitations (for example, they cannot enter into exclusive partnerships nor ensure that any partnership can include all Habitat locations). They also know where there is room for negotiation—for example, in the amount of involvement by the new partner in a specific project's governance and decision making. They assess every potential new partner using the same three broad criteria sets, calling them "deal makers," "deal breakers," and "deal enhancers."

With your position crystal clear, now you'll plan your approach. Start by identifying who should make the initial contact and the message he or she will deliver. It is essential that the individual who makes the approach is able to deliver a concise, high-level message about the opportunity, the value to both companies and the customer, and your willingness to engage with a small senior-level team. It's often effective to request a time frame for a response to a proposal for an exploratory meeting in which both companies can qualify whether the initial concept has enough value, whether it should be modified, or whether there are reasons why the discussions should not proceed at all.

Forming the Alliance

By now we've left the evaluation stage of the process and entered the formation stage. Both sides have agreed that the partnership is a possibility and are ready to seriously explore a potential alliance. But before everyone sits down and negotiates the deal, it's vital to set the stage for a collaborative relationship.

Cisco uses what we call a "shared strategic map" to flesh out, in explicit detail, what the potential partnership will entail so that the parties can learn whether a relationship is mutually beneficial and, if it is, how a potential alliance would operate. Your map should answer such big-picture questions as:

- What is the vision, strategy, and mission of the alliance?

- What is the value proposition for the customer?

- What factors are drawing the companies together? What are the opportunities for collaboration, and what are the potential liabilities?

- Are the two companies' goals aligned? Can their organizations work together effectively?

- What is a possible joint solution? How could it be deployed to the customer?

- Have the companies targeted a specific customer base?

- What is the delivery, service, and support strategy for the joint offering?

- What will constitute success, and how will it be measured? What are the milestones in the relationship?

The key deliverable at this stage is a joint business plan that outlines the opportunity, the assets each company will bring to the relationship, and the investment model that will establish the foundation for the relationship.

The creation of a shared strategic map uncovers the strengths and weaknesses of a potential partnership and makes it apparent whether the two organizations should move forward. A positive answer should solidify and even quantify the case for a partnership—and serve as a springboard as the alliance moves into action.

This is a critical stage for understanding what makes each partner tick. When Cisco first began negotiating with IBM in 1997, both sides realized there was enormous potential. We were already doing business with several IBM units. But there was one stumbling block: IBM had its own networking hardware division that competed with us, although its $400 million in revenues was relatively low compared to our $6.4 billion.

We managed to get the ear of an IBM senior vice president and eventually CEO Lou Gerstner. Gerstner and the senior team knew IBM was not doing well enough to be a long-term player in the networking hardware business. However, they wanted to make sure that working with Cisco created an incremental business opportunity across their divisions, an advantage that would mitigate the business impact of exiting the market. It was only after IBM's leaders came to the conclusion that the opportunity for services, chip sales, and technology licensing would offset their revenue loss that they felt confident enough to move forward into serious discussions. We worked out a deal to take over the networking division's assets, which opened the door to a full-scale agreement. IBM is now Cisco's largest partner, with annual alliance revenues of well over a billion dollars.

When Cisco formed the Italtel alliance by spinning out the product development arm from Telecom Italia, the shared strategic map was quite simple. We wanted a partner who had complementary technology that could help global customers in their transition from time-division switching to packet-switch-based networks and that had a strong local market presence in Italy. Italtel wanted external financing to complete the spinout and a partner who could help the company move the technology into markets outside Italy. Cisco invited in a third-party leveraged-buyout firm as a key financial investor to ensure we had the necessary liquidity.

Doing your due diligence and following a clear process is critical. I inherited one alliance discussion in which we moved ahead *without* doing all the right homework on portfolio overlap. We made premature customer commitments that required us to do the deal, which led to confusion in the field and created significant distrust between the product groups. It took us almost a year to resolve the issues. But it was too late; partner trust had already been damaged. The alliance never recovered its momentum.

You must have the right functions and management levels involved in the alliance so that commitment is threaded throughout the two organizations. In a successful partnership, executives at the highest levels of both companies need to work together and build mutual trust. Identifying the right executive sponsors is key to the relationship's long-term success. Depending on the scope of the relationship, you might have one or two executive sponsors, sometimes engaging both product and sales organizations if the alliance reaches across those functions.

When choosing your executive sponsors, think about the value of the relationship to their business area, and look for overall team chemistry and individuals' willingness to be active participants. Senior executives are usually highly involved with an alliance, with its success factored into part of their job performance. They meet several times a year to review the relationship, set common goals, and resolve challenges. At the executive level, you might need to create a cross-functional global steering committee to help run the relationship, and then regional governance teams that are close to the customer and engaged with their alliance-partner counterparts in a particular market.

Companies too often jump into negotiating the agreement before a draft business plan is complete. This can stymie the process of problem solving and hurt your chances of success. People often stop being creative about how to best address the opportunity, win against the competition, and leverage the assets of both companies. Alliance teams become focused on maximizing their share of the pie rather than on growing the size of the pie itself. At this stage, create agreement around a framework for the necessary components of the alliance, but leave the detailed negotiations for later.

People always ask me, "When do we bring the lawyers into the discussion?"

My answer is simple: sooner rather than later. You'll want your attorneys to spend time listening to and understanding the business discussions and the intent underlying those conversations. That way, they'll be more effective in creating the right legal framework. They'll help you identify potential legal pitfalls, give you ideas about how to structure a deal, and help map out an effective negotiation strategy.

Antitrust issues should certainly be explored early. This is an extremely complicated area of the law and may need to be vetted by an expert in the field.

Another area you'll want counsel on is intellectual property (IP) because virtually all strategic alliances involve some development or licensing of IP rights. IP is governed by a patchwork of laws—copyright, patent, trade secret, trademark—and you'll want to make sure that all the bases are covered. Your attorneys will help you figure out an approach that meets the strategic objectives of the alliance and protects your company's IP assets. I will touch more on that in the discussion of intellectual property in section 5.

You'll also need to work with your lawyers on scoping out the legal and business risks involved in a particular deal. Contractual terms such as limitation of liability, indemnification, warranty disclaimers, and the like are usually vigorously negotiated, and it is best to consider these issues early in the game. You and your attorneys need to come up with a strategy based on your company's risk profile and the value of the particular deal.

Creating a simple contract structure enhances each company's desire to work together to launch and then extend the relationship. What do I mean by "simple contract structure"?

It is something that sets the framework for the alliance and enables this living, breathing organism to continue to flourish. Cisco generally uses a simple framework that includes the following components:

- **Alliance agreement:** Sets the overall aspirations, terms, scope, and governance for the relationship.

- **Joint manufacturing:** Establishes the manufacturing model used by the alliance and the transfer pricing associated with any jointly manufactured products as well as the manufacturing rights held by both companies.

- **Global purchase and supply:** Establishes key terms for the resale of products or services from one company to the other.

- **Joint development agreement:** Outlines the areas of joint development, who will provide what expertise, and the terms and conditions associated with the efforts. This may also address the issue of people engaged in joint development who return to their company and what they can do with the confidential information they acquired from the other company during the joint engagement. It may be appropriate to place restrictions on what types of projects the employee can work on going forward—although such restrictions are not favored under the law and need to be limited in time and scope. The joint development agreement will also articulate how intellectual property will be managed over the course of the relationship. For jointly developed IP, you'll need to agree on ownership. Although joint ownership is a common fallback (and, at first glance, seems the most fair), it often creates more headaches than it's worth. It may make more sense for one of the partners to own the IP (usually the partner for whom the technology is "core"), with responsibility for applying for patents and prosecuting infringers. The other partner then receives a broad license back.

- **Joint marketing agreement:** Usually sets the baseline for the roles and the commitments both companies are making to launch the relationship and the early product offerings.

In these early joint agreements, don't try to assume you know everything. Build a baseline that can be easily modified. The only variable you can be sure of is that these agreements will constantly need changing.

Incubating a Partnership

The shared strategic map gets partners started on the road to collaboration. You next need a map for how you'll work together along the way. We call this the "alliance governance framework" at Cisco. It is the foundation for every alliance.

Structuring the all-important governance agreement is one of the most critical phases of any alliance. I've seen even experienced companies learn the hard way when they try to cut corners in this area.

Eli Lilly comes to mind. Like all big pharmaceutical companies, Lilly needs a steady pipeline of blockbuster new drug discoveries to fuel growth. So it teams up with innovative biotech companies that invent drugs (which Lilly in turn helps fund), move through human trials and FDA approval, and take the drugs to market. For pharmaceutical companies, managing alliances is now as important as building a top-notch in-house research team.

Lilly formed a partnership in 2002 with Amylin Pharmaceuticals to market a potentially revolutionary new diabetes drug, based on a synthetic version of a protein found in the saliva of Gila monsters (yes, Gila monsters). But the two corporate cultures were radically different beasts—Amylin was filled with impulsive, BlackBerry-toting managers, while Lilly's culture was more cautious and relied on low-tech voice-mail communication. The alliance almost melted down, with shouting matches in the hallway and bickering over ways to manufacture a penlike device to deliver the drug.

Lilly's "alliance shrink," Mike Ransom, was eventually called in to rescue the alliance.

That trust was vital as they set up a framework for governing critical decisions. The two teams built trust at an offsite meeting and later broke down tasks and hammered out a detailed plan for areas where one company would take the lead and the other would offer input. Lilly would handle marketing to doctors and consumers, and Amylin would lead education efforts to physicians and patients. In the end, the diabetes drug was submitted to the FDA a year earlier than Lilly had originally thought possible, and it is now undergoing clinical trials.[5]

As this example so painfully illustrates, a governance framework can make or break an alliance. The earlier you put one in place, the better. This framework should outline how the companies will collaborate, communicate, and make decisions once an alliance is under way. In essence, it ties the companies together institutionally, providing multiple points of contact between them.

The framework consists of three major components: alliance management, a decision-making and escalation process, and launching the alliance externally.

Alliance Management

The alliance management team is responsible for ensuring that the partnership runs smoothly on a day-to-day basis. A global alliance director or manager heads the team and is in charge of tracking initiatives, measuring goals, resolving complex issues, and setting strategic activities. Other team members possess the expertise, skills, and commitment to create, market, and sell the joint offerings. The team usually includes people from central marketing and other corporate business units that play critical roles in supporting the alliance. We'll see in the next section how to identify and train the people who will staff the alliance.

A Decision-Making and Escalation Process

With the right team in place, you and your partner need to agree on a systematic structure for making joint decisions. This decision-making capability can help the partnership operate more smoothly and build trust among all the players. If you fail to set up clear decision making in advance of an agreement, you'll create confusion, delay action, and open doors for informal influencers to insert themselves in the process.[6]

A decision-making and escalation process should address:

- How decisions will get made. Will they be decided at the top or pushed down to the lowest levels possible?

- Key decisions to make. What are the top ten to fifteen decisions that the alliance will face first? They might range from long-term contracts to licensing issues.

  A decision map outlines the decision makers and the key decisions they are responsible for that could affect the alliance. Identify even such details as who meets and how often they meet. With our key alliances, we hold meetings between our CEOs about twice a year, executive sponsors meet once a quarter, and alliance and other managers meet as often as once a week.

- Clear escalation paths for problems and issues coming from anywhere in the alliance. You will need multiple paths, depending on the nature of the problem. In the end, executive sponsors—and in some cases, the CEO—will serve as the escalation of last resort.

The Launch of the Alliance Externally

You can use any number of ways to launch an alliance, ranging from major press events to more low-profile approaches, even making no initial announcement at all. But regardless of the method, you absolutely must have clear objectives that underlie the launch. Key issues to factor into the decision include:

- The target audience for any announcement, such as customers, organizations within each company, press and analysts, and so on

- The impact of the announcement on other partners

- Possible competitive reactions

- The field education and customer education you will need

The single biggest mistake you can make is launching before you're ready. Launch prematurely, and you'll sow confusion with your employees and customers and ensure a bad reception from industry and financial analysts. You need to launch the alliance with a clear message about expected value to each company and your mutual customers.

No one size fits all when it comes to incubating an alliance. You have to be flexible enough to allow your alliance teams and stakeholders the freedom to craft the right approach. But with these four elements in place, your alliance will have a much better chance of moving into the marketplace successfully.

Operating the Alliance

You still have work to do after you secure agreement on a governance plan and an operating model. An early step is to jointly create your operating plan. This should be a natural outgrowth of the basic business plan you used to establish the alliance.

Many companies try to tackle too much at first and quickly become overwhelmed. Start with a focused set of initiatives: you need enough projects so that the entire partnership doesn't fall apart when one idea doesn't work out. The initiatives should be balanced, meaning you have some short-term and some long-term wins for both companies. Having only short-term wins may mean you are not looking at the big picture and all the possible game-changing plays, while having only long-term wins may not create the necessary momentum to sustain this living organism through the early stages of its life cycle.

The most common mistakes you can make at this stage are lacking a clear set of criteria that both companies agree on for evaluating initiatives and not staying focused on the activities those priorities support. A lack of decision-making criteria creates circular and often emotional discussions and sometimes encourages the companies involved to try to tackle too many issues as they're still just learning how to work together. You must give your alliance teams some air cover while they go through this vetting process.

In a review of one new partnership, I met with members of the business development teams from both sides and tried to understand their frustrations and lack of progress. After less than a day, it became clear that they had not established mutually clear criteria for evaluating new projects. Management complicated matters by creating a new idea every week for the team to evaluate. Fixing the problem required some pain up front and saying "no" to people at all levels, but we eventually got both sides focused on a balanced set of initiatives and they began making real progress.

One of your big challenges is staying focused. Cisco started one business-planning process with a four-person alliance team that had a list of sixty things it needed to accomplish. The strategy was all over the map. Every vice president in both organizations had added to the list, and naturally, the alliance team was overwhelmed and frustrated. So we sat down with the partner and methodically ranked that company's initiatives and ours against the core goals we had used to establish the relationship. We jointly decided on five efforts we would focus on.

At this stage in the game, it's natural to think the rest is smooth sailing. It's not. In the next step of the operations stage, you need to create and implement the joint product or service. This is a complex and time-consuming stage, but you can make it significantly less cumbersome by following three high-level phases in succession. We call them "concept commit," "execute commit," and "launch commit."

During the concept commit phase, you define and evaluate a specific opportunity with a partner and include an extensive discovery process to explore customer value, the market environment, and risks and barriers to entry. If both sides deem the discovery successful, follow up with an evaluation stage, which should answer such questions as:

- Is there a strategic fit between the companies for this offering?

- Have you defined the target customers and how they will value the combined offering?

- Is the offering technically and operationally feasible within the companies' present business models, or do you need to create a new approach?

- What type of financial benefit or return on investment should the companies expect?

- Is there stakeholder commitment within the companies?

If the concept commit phase yields positive results, you can move on to the execute commit phase. In this stage, you create plans to cover such areas as sales, engineering, testing, support, training, and field engagement.

Finally, in the launch commit phase, you finish marketing plans, legal agreements, and the organizational model. Review the joint business plan to make sure that it's solid and that the teams at both companies are fully staffed and committed. After the exhaustive launch commit phase is complete, partners can confidently begin to market and sell a new joint solution.

To help ensure success with sales, I strongly recommend early field engagement. Bring representatives from the field into the process as early as possible, and keep the sales force fully informed. The sales teams of both companies also should be prepared to collaborate and, if necessary, to change. Kick things off by examining the sales models of the companies. Does each company usually rely on shorter-term or longer-term sales cycles? What is the typical compensation model? Sales-overlay teams can be formed to facilitate collaboration between the partners' sales forces. In the end, you must create sales and compensation models that satisfy all parties, including consultants and resellers.

The last phase of the operations stage involves creating metrics to honestly and openly measure the effectiveness of the partnership. Metrics are the single most important means for managing relationships and raising alliance success rates. They include shared dashboards on operational progress as viewed from each partner's perspective, and both quantitative and qualitative measurements. Going through the process of defining metrics will also help you understand your partner's goals and what's truly important to both companies.

Blue Cross and Blue Shield of Florida (BCBSF) provides health benefits and services to more than 8.6 million people, making it the industry leader in Florida. BCBSF has a team dedicated to alliance management that systematically monitors alliances' contributions to corporate strategies. Team members measure the array of alliances' risk compared to value contribution, distribution of partner organizations, and the contribution to strategic imperatives. Executives regularly review alliances' strategic, financial, operational, and relationship performance throughout the year. The team can show its executives that more than 80 percent of BCBSF's alliances meet or exceed targeted strategic and financial results. Annual surveys of alliance partners consistently show that 85 percent or more view BCBSF as a "partner of choice" and that 86 percent or better say they receive significant value through their alliance with BCBSF.

For many partnerships, the most important metric will be the number of bookings and amount of revenue a joint product or service produces. In addition, other significant metrics may include:

- Has the alliance produced cost savings for either company in its value chain through such things as reduced R&D or lower cost of sales, manufacturing, customer support, or service?

- How many new sales engagements have resulted from the partnership?

- How has the relationship evolved at the executive and alliance levels? Has communication been clear? Have meetings been productive? Have important issues been resolved satisfactorily?

- Are both companies continuing to add value to the alliance? Are they increasing their resource allocation, investment, expertise, or training in the joint product or service? Have they met past benchmarks?

- What joint products or services are planned for the future?

Don't be afraid to think outside the box: metrics can—and should be—creative. When the California-based Peninsula Beverly Hills hotel teamed up with Toyota, it kept a close eye on performance. The hotel offered free use of a Lexus to guests who stayed in its luxury suites. Toyota benefited from the introduction of its new luxury sedan to an affluent group of customers. Metrics of tangible benefits included the number of large-suite reservations and the number of guests who requested the use of a Lexus. Measures of intangible benefits included customer satisfaction as gauged from surveys.[7]

Whatever metrics you choose, these goals should be documented and publicized within both companies *before* the launch. Based on solid information, you can then judge what's working, what's not working, and where you need to make resource adjustments. The information also will help ensure continued stakeholder support and alignment of business goals. You'll find that shared metrics are one of the most important ways to get everyone on the same page and to communicate more broadly the results of the relationship.

Transitioning or Retiring the Alliance

Naturally, things change: the goals of an alliance may evolve as results point to areas for improvement. In other words, alliances often need a tune-up to update strategic goals and reconfirm a joint commitment. This process can also point out when the time is ripe to retire an alliance. For that, you'll also need a plan and a process to unwind the deal in an orderly fashion (more on that in section 4).

The desire to end an alliance can start with a change of business strategy or an acquisition or another partnership that alters the landscape; the need could also arise because the partnership is not producing the required results because of changing market conditions—or simply because of an inability to work together as companies. For any of these reasons, this stage is extremely hard to execute because it often means addressing the fact that the alliance has not succeeded. But you must manage it like any other phase of the life cycle.

You have two fundamental options at this point. You can focus the relationship on a more limited area, such as a simple business relationship between the respective areas of each company's business. There's nothing wrong with resetting the goals to something that still brings value to both companies but may not be as broad and as visible as the relationship had been initially envisioned. The other option is to retire the alliance, terminating the agreement and many of the ongoing business development and customer engagements associated with the partnership. This decision is more difficult and has a greater probability of significant damage if not performed carefully.

Retiring an alliance correctly requires you to execute on several critical components: protections for your mutual customers, stakeholder buy-in from within your company, and clear communication to the groups involved in the alliance. At this point, you need to manage any emotional reaction and keep your eye on the ball. The world continues to change, and you never know when a new opportunity may arise that could give both companies a good reason to work together in the future. How you separate can have significant implications for your reputation as a potential partner and with your customers, so make the parting professional.

We terminated our strategic-alliance relationship with Ericsson because of its acquisition strategy, which we felt created significant competitive technology overlap, compromised growth opportunities, and put our field sales and services organizations into conflicting positions in front of the customers. We unwound the deal only after we had made sure we could service our mutual customers and after a careful scenario analysis of the upsides and downsides of continuing or terminating the relationship. We also made it a point to sit down with Ericsson and review all the alternatives and the rationale for our decision. We have implemented a program where we still work together tactically, case-by-case, driven by local customer needs. There was complete buy-in from both of our teams because they played a key part in the analysis.

Not even the best system can ensure success. As we've learned in this section, the right framework can create an environment that fuels collaboration and builds trust—the foundation of all alliances. Yet to achieve a successful alliance, you must have the right people on board. They have to be carefully trained and managed. That's what we'll explore in the next section.

Developing the Right Organization

In the best-selling book *Good to Great*, Jim Collins introduces the idea of "First Who . . . Then What." Rather than obsessing over crafting the perfect vision or strategy statement, great companies focus on getting the right people on the bus and in the right seats, and getting the wrong people off the bus. Only then do they figure out where to drive it.

It turns out that having the right people on board, and the right leader at the wheel, scored higher than any measure, including compensation, in helping companies make the leap from good to great. Forget the old adage "People are your most important asset." Instead, the *right people* are your most important asset. This is a team-based approach, as opposed to the model of the "genius with a thousand helpers," which is built around the talents of one extraordinary individual.[8]

But let me take Collins's idea one step further. Not only do you need to put the right people in place; they need to be the right ones for building alliances. And you'll need to develop alliance all-stars—no other investment is as important. Skimp in this area, and you'll fall flat on your face.

Identifying the Key Skills of a Great Alliance Leader

I view alliance managers like orchestra conductors: they get all the players playing the right notes at the right time. Alliance conductors craft a compelling business plan, get executive buy-in up and down the chain of command, and work with business units and salespeople to execute on the strategy. Your managers also have to know the strengths and weaknesses of each partner, understand the products intimately, and ensure that the team gets the resources it needs to follow through on the plan. They connect all the dots—and drive the alliance forward.

IBM has two thousand employees who have the word "alliance" in their titles, although there is not a consistent definition of an alliance manager across the organization. IBM has said that the most important traits an alliance manager can possess are market intelligence, a global perspective, an understanding of different business models, and knowing how to bring together complex technologies to create value for customers.[9]

Alliance managers at Cisco operate at the nexus of strategy, sales, and technology. They must understand how to derive value from a relationship; analyze the strengths and weaknesses of both partners to determine who does what; understand how the alliance partners' products and services can work together; and develop new products. They also need to have the people skills to sell these products both upward to the relevant executives and downward to the salespeople who eventually have to sell the joint products.

These leaders live in limbo, with little official power and ambiguous roles. Their jobs can be lonely outposts in many cases. They must be the internal advocate, external promoter, chief relationship builder, and master of personal influence. Their job is to identify the strategic value proposition between the companies and, at the end of the day, to be able to cultivate sponsors on both sides.

You usually don't find these characteristics in a college recruit. In a study of more than forty U.S. companies that use strategic alliances, the beginning alliance managers had an average of ten years of experience when they joined the alliance team.[10]

"The goal of the alliance manager is not to create harmony but to create a sense of dynamic tension," relates one CEO with a diverse portfolio of alliances. "Think of the cathedral at Notre Dame with its flying buttresses. It is the equal and opposing pressure that keeps it up. That is the basic architecture inside the alliance."[11]

Managers must also be able to run their organization like a business, with a board, a business plan, and a staff who deal with sales, delivery, execution, and other areas. At Cisco, we like to say that we have 150 alliance team members who leverage thousands of people across all functions in the company.

Alliance leaders in your organization have little power except what they can muster through personal influence. A lot of people, especially at lower levels, ask me again and again, "What do you guys do exactly?" Overworked salespeople may be skeptical of the alliance role, challenging managers by asking, "What's in it for me?" Many large organizations have flat hierarchies, and people at middle levels, particularly salespeople, can have a surprising degree of power. Their arms can't easily be twisted, even by people at a higher rank.

There's nothing easy about this job; it's complex and always changing. To handle the demands, you need to identify a unique blend of skills and knowledge. In addition to leadership and other general management skills, look for seven basic characteristics when screening senior alliance candidates:

- **Cross-functional experience:** You need versatile leaders, with hard business know-how as well as softer general management capabilities. Some organizations look at people who have worked at jobs that cross the value chain as a liability. The thinking is that they're not focused. But experience across business functions like sales, marketing, management, and product development is essential to making a great alliance manager. The experience gives such managers an appreciation for each organization and each function's role in making an alliance work.

- **Ability to synthesize quickly:** Someone who can operate at a high level and think quickly on his or her feet is a must. An alliance manager often has to take a complex series of activities and issues and make it simple for everyone to understand how to resolve an issue. One of Cisco's best strategic alliance leaders was a former CEO of a small company.

Many times you will be given a limited window to talk with senior people or review possible ideas when reasonably quick action will either create or kill an opportunity.

- **Multimode communication skills:** Your leaders must have excellent written and verbal communication skills and be comfortable working at all levels within both organizations. They should be able to create a message suitable and understandable for a CEO or an individual contributor within any functional group.

- **Strategically relevant knowledge:** An alliance leader does not have to design products but must understand the market environment in which the company operates, the benefits of the capabilities each company offers, and how to align companies to create incremental opportunity for both sides.

- **Global experience and sensitivity:** Most large businesses now derive a significant percentage of revenues from outside the United States. Leaders now need experience working around the world, as well as an appreciation for a wide range of cultures and market environments.

- **Ability to work in unstructured and ambiguous environments:** By its very nature, the alliance role offers a tremendous variety of activities and endless options when looking for ways to create value. In an unstructured environment, you need someone who is disciplined, can set clear priorities with the key stakeholders, and knows how to say "no." Symptoms of poor alliance management include too many initiatives on the table, lack of completion of key focus areas, and a frustrated partner.

- **Emotional balance and self-confidence:** Look for people who have demonstrated their ability to handle constant setbacks and rejections. It's not an easy job, and only certain types are cut out for it. They must be driven and motivated by more than money. I've observed over the years that the best alliance managers are motivated by the opportunity to do something different, to create something new that can't be done by either company alone, and to bring value to the market. Good alliance managers are secure enough to give credit to other organizations, relying on the respect of their peers and senior executives to feed their egos.

Creating a Winning Alliance
Environment with People Skills

Knowing how to deal with people at all levels to help create collaborative win-win environments isn't an innate skill set in many corporations, where a Darwinian win-at-any-cost approach often prevails. But it's essential for building relationships that stand the test of time.

You must find managers who are able to understand the executives in their own companies—those executives' decision-making styles, their perspectives on change, the personal and professional experiences that shape their view of their world, their knowledge of the subject, and their spheres of influence. Such managers must be able to influence higher-ups' key influencers—before any important decision can get made.

Diplomacy is another key part of the alliance team's mission. Your leaders should have the ability to work internally with executive sponsors and all their direct reports, as well as to intuitively understand how each one thinks and how something might fit into that person's strategy. Such leaders must also be able to reach out to dozens of managers and get them to go along—even though they have no power over them. And they must be in constant communication with their external counterparts, playing the diplomat at every level.

Broad and deep personal relationships across organizations make this kind of open communication second nature. In many companies, it's often as much *who* you know as *what* you know. I've found that a sense of personal gravitas helps enormously in building relationships. Successful leaders are comfortable talking with people at all levels of the organization, but especially with top executives. They have a personal style that motivates executives to return their calls and show up at important meetings.

But finding the right people requires that you first ask some hard questions about your talent-management systems and processes:

- Does your company understand the skills and responsibilities needed for a successful alliance manager?

- What are you doing to attract top talent to your alliance organization?

- How do you differentiate manager roles, such as operations and relationship building?

- Is alliance management a legitimate career path in your company?

You'll probably find alliance expertise scattered across pockets of your company. Think through how you're going to pull that together. You may need to break down silos and encourage information sharing, as we'll see later.

Growing Your Staff and Helping Them Grow

You can't just make the right hires and pat yourself on the back. You also need to continuously develop your staff's skills.

But before you jump into setting up a training program, step back and think about what you're training people *for*. The process starts with something as simple sounding as creating a detailed job description.

This job profile serves as a blueprint for how to become more effective in a job and how best to grow and advance. You need to offer a clear picture of which activities are normally performed in a job, the deliverables that are expected, the ways in which managers can measure their proficiency, and the skills that will contribute to success as they grow and strengthen their proficiency in key areas.

Be sure to design an alliance manager profile to allow growth from those early in their roles through to the most senior members of the team. As individuals advance, core competencies shift from managing existing alliance initiatives to increasing levels of cross-functional and innovative finesse.

Think about organizing job descriptions around four areas: responsibilities, outputs, metrics, and skills. Detail them so that you make performance expectations explicit, objectively measure performance, and reward top performers with advancement.

Responsibilities are the critical activities that are expected from a role and are presented as clusters of tasks or job activities. These can be broken up into core, advanced, and most senior levels. (See figure 2 in the appendix.) For example, a new Cisco alliance professional would be expected to manage an established alliance initiative, while a senior alliance manager should create breakthrough opportunities.

Outputs are the tangible products of a job responsibility or, in other words, the deliverables that a manager might be asked to produce. They answer the question, "What am I expected to deliver in this job?" (See figure 3 in the appendix.) Again, expectations vary based on the experience and skill level of an alliance manager.

Metrics help assess the quality of outcomes and responsibilities. I've identified some of the main indicators that we use at Cisco to gauge the effectiveness of managers in their roles. (See figure 4 in the appendix.) Metrics answer the question, "How do I measure success?"

Skills are capabilities, knowledge, and personal attributes that contribute to an individual's success in a particular job or business situation. It's the *how* of the job and answers the question, "What do I need to allow me to succeed?" (See figure 5 in the appendix.)

Developing an Education Strategy for Your Alliance Organization

Now let's push Collins's logic another step. Once you've put the right people in place, what are you doing to help them achieve *personal* greatness? Through training and education, you'll develop managers *and* hold them to the highest standards.

And here you can't just rely on your own corporate education organization—you have to take control and invest in a wide range of internal training and education.

The problem is that training across U.S. companies is low by global standards. In Asia, companies spend twice as much on training as a percentage of payroll.[12] And until the past few years, there was little formal training for alliance managers. Only one-third of companies surveyed by Booz Allen Hamilton offered alliance training, and fewer than 15 percent had developed their own curriculum.[13]

You may be tempted to rely on your corporate education organization to offer a few courses here and there. Alternatively, managers can learn by trial and error as they go or take outside courses from experts. But in each case, the learning won't be as deep or as relevant as you need it to be.

There's a better way. Leaders in the alliances field— like Eli Lilly, Dow Corning, Cisco, and others—often deploy a systematic, scalable process for education and training, built on consistency and best practices. High-performing alliance organizations specifically develop and train their managers as a matter of course.

Dow has a long history of joint ventures and minority equity positions, but a strategic review uncovered islands of expertise. There was no central place for shared knowledge about best practices. So Dow created an interactive alliance course that has so far trained more than two hundred managers and has helped shape upwards of twenty deals worth more than $2 billion in market value. Courses are supplemented with an online knowledge base available twenty-four hours a day around the world.[14]

BellSouth created a two-day, cross-functional alliance workshop for 150 of its senior managers. Among the lessons it gleaned from the experience was that people learn from each other and that defined processes work. And Nortel created a training program after one alliance failed, building the program on organizational planning, three-day workshops, and networking.[15]

At Cisco, we built our training program on three broad areas:

- Staff management and team-building competencies—like performance management, coaching, managing virtual and global teams—always being careful to link strategy to job requirements

- Functional skills like negotiation, go-to-market planning, market sector knowledge, and a fluency with regulatory standards

- General management capabilities like scenario planning, problem solving and complex decision making, scaling business opportunities, strategy alignment, and financial acumen

We also stress our thirty best practices, developing training for each of these areas. And we're working with the Association of Strategic Alliance Professionals to promote education standards and to develop a global certification program. We hope to elevate the alliance manager to a higher professional standard and create a versatile program that can adapt to a rapidly changing world.

You can start down this path by convening senior managers to think through, at a high level, how they want to organize an education program. Articulate coverage areas, knowledge gaps to address, and the stages of an alliances career path. Then identify what you expect in a high-performing alliance leader. What skills are needed in the job at different levels as managers move up the ladder? You want to develop a career path from alliance manager to director to vice president. Every company is different, so it's important to relate expectations with the company culture, as well.

You also want to explore how training ties into the mission of the strategic alliance organization. The alliance manager is a position that can vary based on the type of alliance being managed. Larger alliances will generally allow for greater specialization of responsibilities, whereas smaller alliances will draw on a broad range of skills.

Making Education Second Nature

Once you've carefully thought through your expectations for team members and how you'll use training strategically, you'll want to develop an ongoing education program to help managers master their responsibilities and outputs; the program can also help them achieve their performance metrics and develop their skills, no matter what level they're at. This, of course, takes planning, investment, and time. But the payoff is well worth it, and we've found that off-the-shelf courses are not usually sufficient for this level of alliance training.

Cisco offers one- to three-day workshops for a wide range of alliance management topics. These classes go beyond what's normally presented in a corporate education course. We have a set of ongoing foundation courses with required attendance for all alliance team members and then selected courses that we rotate every twelve to twenty-four months based on senior management agreement about the evolving needs of the broader team.

The Self-Developing Organization (SDO) is one of our foundational courses. It's a three-day leadership workshop that links strategy to problem solving and is based on three principle objectives: taking responsibility for your career and growth in alliances, understanding the cross-functional dependencies of your relationships, and understanding the critical importance of multilevel communications.

The class uses techniques such as a computer-simulation program that lets participants run a company like Cisco and an exercise demonstrating the huge impact that poor communication can have on a team. In the three-day simulation exercise, managers hear from an array of speakers, such as senior business-unit managers or strategists within the company; each day represents a business year in the simulation. About thirty alliance managers break up into groups and make decisions that include product functionality, hiring, and partner strategy. Attendees are evaluated on how well they managed partner strategy, generated partner alignment, and understood the complex interrelations.

Managers know that being able to influence and build relationships is a core skill. The SDO workshops go beyond typical communication-training events to show how to build a "circle of influence" to gain the support of people from different backgrounds and personalities—everyone from a highly logical engineer to a hard-charging salesperson.

Another class focuses on leading complex negotiations. We found that standard negotiation classes were too basic for building complex relationships, so Cisco developed a class that drills down deeper. These two- to three-day workshops stress creating win-win solutions, rather than winner-take-all outcomes. We encourage managers to think about negotiations as if they were talking with their family: you have to worry about long-term relationships.

We build gut-level comprehension—not just cognitive awareness—of the critical principles, behavior, and techniques of high-performing negotiators by immersing participants in engaging and powerful simulations. The class employs a full-spectrum approach through competitive, collaborative, and creative negotiation skills that protect company interests, build relationships, break deadlocks, and lead to more profitable solutions. We emphasize strategies for making concessions, with particular emphasis on uncovering what we call "elegant negotiables" and avoiding costly concessions throughout the interaction.

For the upper-level management teams, we are building training that applies some of the scenario-planning tools to both individual and portfolio alliance management.

Meanwhile, alliance managers are indoctrinated on the thirty-point strategic alliance life cycle—the bible in our organization—through courses and online knowledge banks. One online resource allows managers to click on any one of thirty stages and view a presentation or on-demand video. We have created a best-practice virtual team from across the organization that reviews all best-practice submissions each quarter and determines winners. This serves the purpose of both recognizing outstanding performers and their ideas and using the virtual team to spread the news across the organization. Alliance team members who suggest a best practice receive kudos in quarterly all-hands meetings, are recognized online, and the finalists receive a monetary award.

Eli Lilly is ahead of the game with its online partners database, which includes contracts, governance information, and progress reports about each alliance. The database supports Lilly's educational efforts with best practices about what has worked for its hundred-plus partnerships with innovative biotech companies. These lessons help it avoid the organizational, technological, and governance pitfalls that can derail an alliance.[16]

In fact, a study by Booz Allen Hamilton found that successful alliance organizations are twice as likely as unsuccessful companies to have built an online repository of alliance knowledge and information, and that the content is dramatically richer.

None of this is easy, of course, and you must keep in mind that your education effort will face many roadblocks in designing effective programs. To achieve success, keep the following in mind:

- The content must clearly tie in with strategy and the daily work of the alliance manager, and it must be relevant.

- Cross-functional learning doesn't happen automatically—people are naturally siloed.

- This is a long-term process, not an overnight project.

Learning Outside the Classroom

Ultimately, the goal of training is to develop a well-rounded alliance leader who can operate across many environments. But not everything can be learned in a classroom. A great deal of learning takes place in the real world, where applying what you have learned provides the true test.

Through coaching and collaboration, alliance managers can learn from one other. But there's often a big hurdle: most don't think to share; they're buried in their own alliance and too busy to share best practices or information. You have to tackle this issue head-on. Focus on breaking down functional and alliance silos and creating an atmosphere in which alliance managers can share information and work together. Consider forming virtual teams that focus on activities that span organizations and functions, such as emerging trends and product areas.

You should also tap your veteran managers to help. Consider recruiting them to act as coaches or mentors, perhaps assigning them to the newest managers. Cisco is just starting to experiment with a program to rotate managers into different alliances after two or three years. The idea is that managers can fall into a career rut if they work on only one type of alliance. So moving them from, say, a big technology alliance like Intel into a partnership with a system integrator like Accenture will make them more well rounded.

On a broader scale, each alliance deal should be viewed as a learning opportunity. Companies often team up to learn new manufacturing techniques. But they can also share learning and best practices. Part of the value of alliances is how much knowledge you can capture. Learn from your partners.

This goes back to the collaborative mind-set of win-win negotiations. When we were struggling with a partnership with EDS a few years ago, we developed a two-day workshop to train our teams together. Alliance managers, salespeople, and senior executives all attended, and we rolled up our sleeves and really dug into how Cisco views alliance management. We reviewed our best practices, techniques, and overall approach. It helped the teams cohere better and helped the EDS team come up to speed on our practices.

Going Global

Today's alliance environment is all about change on a global scale. You can build a more global organization using four fundamental strategies:

- **The lead-follow model:** An alliance can be run from anywhere in the world, and the other geographic sectors can follow. You should put your alliance team members where it makes the most sense relative to the purpose of the alliance and the needs of the partner.

- **Core competency centers:** Our alliance organization has three geographically based centers staffed with people representing more than twelve nationalities. We have to distribute our resources globally but like to cluster skills, where possible, to get critical mass.

- **Staff rotation:** Consider an international rotation program in which a select number of employees are moved from region to region.

- **Advanced collaboration tools:** We use secure Web sites to provide information on our activities and plans. We are also scaling our use of the latest in collaboration tools, such as Cisco's TelePresence rooms, to change how we work globally within our team and with our partners, including executive governance reviews.

Once you've got the right people in place on your alliance team, it's imperative that you be rigorous and creative in developing them. Many companies simply don't invest enough in this area, and then they wonder why their alliances fail to prosper. The smart companies go the extra mile and invest heavily in their employees. Employ any and all moves in your playbook, and be prepared to invent new ones.

Building a great alliance organization means you must never quit innovating or investing in leadership development. The sooner you start, the better. This work will strengthen not just your people but, as we'll see in the next section, the relationships they form with your partners.

Building the Right
Relationships

You can have the best process and people in the world, but an alliance can still go painfully wrong. So frequently in business, it comes down to the *relationships* between partners. Building and maintaining these connections requires soft skills that are hard to teach and difficult to quantify, but invaluable.

Relationships are the art of the alliance. They are also the glue that holds an alliance together, particularly when conflicts break out. You must make building strong relationships an essential part of every alliance or risk watching it implode at the first sign of discord. Contrary to popular belief at many companies, legal agreements can't run the day-to-day business of an alliance or legislate human behavior. Formal processes are helpful, but they can't substitute for the hard work of getting to know people, developing connections, and building trust.

In a three-year study of alliance managers at 130 companies, Vantage Partners found that over half of those interviewed reported that "poor or damaged relationships" were the primary cause of alliance failure. The damage was marked by breakdowns in trust, suspicions over partners' motives, festering conflicts, and strong feelings of disrespect.

And the more alliances a company formed, the lower its relationship management capabilities often rated. Two-thirds of failures were the result of soured relationships at companies with more than twenty alliances.[17]

In other words, it isn't bad strategy or poor legal advice that dooms most partnerships. It's the leaders' inability to get along and maintain a level of trust. It can take months or years to build trust, but just moments to break it. This is complicated by the fact that business relationships can often feel more like family or personal relationships—messy, complex, and often emotionally charged.

The good news is that you *can* manage relationships with the right blend of art and science: with first-rate people skills and a systematic process for strengthening connections. This section outlines strategies for developing relationships that enable alliances to weather the inevitable storms of conflict.

We've seen the importance of relationships time and again in Cisco's alliances. As one example, we have a partnership with IBM that embeds Cisco products into the large technology integration and service offerings that IBM delivers. We've built our business relationship slowly over a decade, and the companies have fostered a high-level relationship between their respective CEOs. Today the partnership is worth more than $1 billion in revenues for both sides.

Cisco has succeeded with such alliances by building relationships that will survive conflicts—and we've had our share. We've managed these using techniques like common dashboards, clear governance models, and regular quarterly reviews, along with social activities like dinners, which enable personal relationships to develop. We've also employed clear escalation models for rapid trouble resolution and other vehicles for steady, ongoing communication.

The lesson is simple: strategic alliances are more than just legal contracts. They're living, dynamic relationships between real people. At the end of the day, many crises can be solved with just a few key phone calls and discussions—if you have strong relationships. But you must develop them right from the beginning.

Building Trust in the Early Days

In the previous section, we explored how the right people instinctively know ways to build relationships and trust. Alliance managers are like social chameleons. These leaders have to be great communicators who are able to talk to everyone from the janitor to the CEO. It takes a special breed of person to develop and manage relationships at this level.

Once you've found these people and put the right overall alliance process in place, you need to forge rock-solid relationships with your colleagues on the other side. This may sound blindingly obvious, but I've encountered few people who truly understand the dynamics and meaning of these connections. Relationships must be as carefully thought through and as well executed as any product plan.

It starts with a unique mind-set even before the first negotiation, which often serves as the foundation for the alliance. Think in terms of win-win negotiations and what's in it for "we" versus "me." Big companies are often accustomed to calling the shots and will go to the mat to protect their interests. It's all about "me." But when you're truly collaborating, "me" becomes "we": rather than saying, "I did that," skillful relationship builders say, "We did that."

There's a time and place to think of your own agenda, of course. In the negotiation stage of any alliance, it's essential that you be firm about your needs and priorities. In a straightforward and honest way, you must explain how your partner fits into your strategy and how both companies can benefit not just now but over the long term. If you're choosing a company because it allows you access to a new market or a new distribution channel, or it fits within your company's long-term strategy in some way, make that clear.

But you must also take the time to learn your partners' real goals and ambitions and to understand what really makes them tick, philosophically and culturally. Are they risk averse, while you're used to flying by the seat of your pants? Are they planners, while you're doers?

You've got to push beyond the other side's stated positions to uncover that company's unexpressed, deeply held fears and interests. You have to be soft on the people while still negotiating hard on the substance. Demonstrate your understanding of your prospective partner's position, and show in concrete ways that you can be trusted. Several times at Cisco, we've opted to concede on specific points during the negotiations—not because we thought we'd lose, but because we wanted to demonstrate that the long-term relationship was more important than maximizing the value of our position. Your prospective partner has to believe the scales are balanced, or the partnership will be short lived. You can win the negotiation and lose the alliance before you even start.

This is all Negotiations 101 for the most experienced people in your organization. But it's not necessarily second nature to those you lead; it has to be modeled and taught, as shown in the previous section.

What's more advanced is the process by which excellent negotiators structure partnerships to specifically *protect and strengthen* relationships. Contracts naturally need to support what you're trying to do in the business, but they must also include enough flexibility for your managers to build relationships and adapt as the business changes on the ground.

You need to create systems for managing relationships and conflict early on. Take the time to learn how your partner makes decisions, resolves conflict, and handles change, and compare these characteristics to your own organization. What kind of vocabulary or product lingo does the other company use, and how can you bridge that communication divide? Figure out your partner's track record of managing relationships to predict likely pitfalls ahead.

Then put all this information on the table, and explore how the relationship will need to work for both sides to feel comfortable and handle the inevitable challenges you'll face together. Define a set of relationship roles and structures. Which levels of each organization will need to work together, and how? Your director may need to talk to the other company's senior vice president, and both sides will need to break down the inevitable hierarchical walls that can so easily impede communication. When devising a communication structure, be sure to:

- Agree in advance on five to ten key decisions— including transfer pricing, staffing, capital expenditures, and investments—that are key to the alliance during the first twelve months. The time spent up front on these areas will uncover points of conflict and prevent misunderstandings in the future.

- Create a decision-making map assigning key players at both companies to those important decisions, and detail their level of involvement, such as consultation only or actual decision making. Make sure that these people get to know each other early on, both professionally and socially, and that they understand the importance of their roles in helping the alliance in the early stages of the relationship.

- Build conflict-resolution systems that clearly identify the escalation paths and expectations on the speed of this escalation, based on the severity of the issue.

- Have a framework to deal with any serious changes in the assumptions underlying the alliance. The framework should facilitate in-depth discussions focused on any effects from the changes and predefined ways to resolve them if they involve long-term investments. Mechanisms can be created to rebalance ownership if one side turns out to be investing more heavily than the other. If you're unable to agree on key terms, you and your partner should part ways and divide control over certain segments of the business.

Building the Relationship over Time

Building connections with partners is about creating a web of interwoven connections—the more connections, the stronger the web. To build a bridge to people at another company, you need to create the right environment.

Dozens of players at all levels must be involved. Typically, only a few core people at the executive level will have bonded over the formation of a deal. But many other people must now be brought along and imbued with the same level of enthusiasm and understanding of the deal's advantages for them. Remember that many people inside and outside your organization can create roadblocks if they aren't brought in early and often. Leaders of strong independent business units can undermine a relationship, for instance, because their interests don't always align with those of the company as a whole.

You can't just tell people what to do. They're told to do a million things a day. All things being equal, they will talk to someone they know and like rather than just another business colleague.

To build this level of rapport, you need to carefully match roles and cultures. As part of the governance process, regular meetings are critical to keep communication flowing. And for that, you need to match up executives at the same level across functions and geographies to ensure ongoing focus and commitment to the relationship. For global relationships, we have a global governing body, including sales, services, and technology groups. For each sales region in which the alliance operates, there are matching executives who drive the strategy and activities in that region. In some cases, because Cisco's regions don't exactly map to a partner's, we will combine governance reviews with our counterparts.

Matching the culture of two companies is not always easy. Cisco isn't as hierarchical as other big companies and has fewer layers of management, which makes matching up executives challenging. Whereas many large companies have many executive and senior vice presidents, Cisco only has about forty senior vice presidents and five executive vice presidents. A senior director has as much authority at Cisco as a VP at many other big companies, and we frequently match up executives at this level to work together on day-to-day issues and at quarterly meetings; this is easier said than done in many cases. The issue is not matching the title but matching the scope of responsibilities and personalities of the people involved.

I was engaged in one partnership where I was working with all vice presidents; I was a senior director at the time. For the first few months, I was mystified that these senior managers wouldn't return any of my phone calls. I learned it was completely hierarchical; they wouldn't talk to anyone below VP level. So at one of our alliance reviews, I commented about the situation to their alliance leader, "This is a big problem because I'm empowered to represent Cisco on these things, and I can't get responses from any of your team. I'm convinced it has nothing to do with me personally, but they don't believe in your culture that by talking to me, a senior director, something's going to happen. They think this is a senior vice president issue for our company."

He responded directly: "We'll fix this. At our next major customer event, I want you there, and I want you at my table with my biggest customers." When everyone on his management team saw me sitting next to him at the table, talking to him and all these customers, the problem was solved instantly.

Ideally, you want to match up people who have similar roles and a similar culture. We call it "impedance matching." For instance, we'll try to match our head of sales operations with someone at the partner company who owns sales operations. This can be a challenge. The company may call the position "head of delivery," or the role might be combined with business development. Be open and creative with the match. Your peer may not be at the exact same level, but he or she may still be the right match. Look past the organization chart, and go with your instincts.

Matching cultures is even harder than matching roles. When Cisco teamed up with Fujitsu, it was clear to Cisco's alliance team that a partnership would speed the company's entry into the vital networking market in Japan, where customers were on the cutting edge of technology adoption but often preferred to buy domestic products. Meanwhile, Fujitsu was looking for a strong technology supplier.

The process of hammering out an agreement required nine months, much of it spent figuring out the best route to market. Even though Cisco already had its own sales office in Japan, it became clear that the highest chance of success would come through a collaborative effort that combined Cisco's technology with Fujitsu's route to the customer. Fujitsu even agreed to put its engineers, donning Cisco identification badges, on the project to jointly create the core routers.

Alliance managers were the secret ingredient for this successful partnership. Throughout, they played diplomat between two companies with radically different cultures. While Cisco's managers are comfortable calling up someone two levels above to brief them on a meeting, this practice is frowned on in Japan. The Japanese system is much more hierarchical. And the typical American approach of trying to bulldoze your position through a negotiation would have failed. Cisco's managers respected Fujitsu's way of doing things and attuned themselves to creating cross-cultural chemistry and building trust.

When matching cultures, you have to create translation mechanisms to bridge the divide. Sometimes two companies will say the same thing, but each will mean something different. You have to develop a vocabulary and understanding of how the other company uses terms and how its people think about their business aspirations. Here the alliance team can play the critical role of translator, saying, "Well, this is what they really mean when they say this." In one case we actually had to create a simple, common set of definitions and training programs addressing cultural differences after discovering that each company interpreted similar statements differently. This problem is most common—but not exclusive to—relationships spanning different countries and cultures.

Regular forums for communication are vital to keeping everyone on the same page and the relationships functioning well. In all our governance structures, we make sure we spell out how often the parties need to be in communication, follow-up protocols, and who needs to be talking to whom.

Managing Conflicts

Conflicts can occur across the spectrum of a working relationship: product development schedules, sales, technical standards, money. Mistrust can ultimately explode into a vicious cycle of recriminations.

Past relationship breakdowns can also create huge hurdles for future collaboration. Sometimes when we talk with a Cisco salesperson about cooperating with an alliance partner, the salesperson will say, "No way. That company played games with us in the past."

A rocky history played a part in the case of the Eli Lilly and Amylin Pharmaceuticals alliance, which we mentioned in section 2. Amylin had been burned in earlier partnerships with bigger partners and was leery of entering into the agreement with Eli Lilly, making it hard to build any trust. The agreement called for Amylin to jointly develop and commercialize a diabetes drug, Exenatide, for which it received up-front payments and additional payments later, once the drug was introduced worldwide. But the alliance was rife with infighting and conflicts from the beginning: Amylin felt that Lilly was constantly butting in and didn't trust the giant company in the long term, fearing it would bail out if the results from final trials came up short.

The alliance was saved when fifty Lilly and Amylin managers were brought together for two days of team building at a hotel in Dallas. They took personality tests and worked on shared goals, and there were even dance parties and social gatherings. It took months, but the two sides finally broke the ice and started to trust each other. That led to Lilly pumping more money into the alliance and cleanly working out the separation of roles and responsibilities, eventually leading to a successful partnership.[18]

Save yourself some grief, and lay this kind of groundwork early so you can manage conflicts *before* they erupt. You have to take the lead and set the tone rather than wait for your partner, using the right process and versatile people skills. Outlined below are three suggested tips: relationship maps, common dashboards, and two-way early-warning systems.

- **Relationship maps:** We mitigate against conflicts through a regular audit of our partner relationship and governance model called a "relationship map." This map provides a semi-annual review of the people side of the relationship. Simply put, it forces us to review key issues that could make or break our relationships:

  - First, given the critical decisions required to operate the relationship, we make sure we have individuals identified at both companies who are accountable for those decisions.

  - Second, we use a simple stoplight chart to indicate the status of that relationship. It's a formal element of science that we inject into the relationship-building game. Specific relationship parameters are judged and assigned a status of green, yellow, or red. Yellow or red status indicates that issues in the relationship need to be addressed.

- **Common dashboards:** We also try and make sure that both companies have created a common dashboard to measure mutual success so there is minimal confusion when a real problem emerges. In one partnership, our dashboard was flashing red in certain areas based on our understanding of issues such as the mutual customer's satisfaction and quality of delivery. But our partner's dashboard indicated everything was running smoothly, reflecting a successful relationship. We learned we had two different dashboards. We met with the other company's team, reviewed the discrepancies and overall partnership, and combined these into one dashboard. This gave us a unified view on measuring success, which led to our executives coming together.

At the end of the day, managing conflicts simply involves being honest and having integrity. When something goes wrong—say, one company makes a deal that impacts its partner negatively—successfully preserving the relationship hinges on the strength of the bonds. Many times I've seen it come down to a phone call between three or four people and how they manage the conflict.

- **Two-way early-warning systems:** Providing advanced communications to your partner and alerting its team members to potentially bad news (or news that can be interpreted in different ways) is absolutely critical to maintaining strong people bonds; this is the fabric that holds the relationship together. On the flip side, when your partner makes a potentially negative move, you must be able to rapidly analyze and disseminate news to key people in your company.

There are three key techniques you need to consider to avoid unnecessary confusion or loss of trust when it comes to communication. First, make sure your alliance organization is plugged into the corporate communications and mergers-and-acquisitions (M&A) teams within your company. Use your early-warning system to alert key players to potentially disruptive moves. Cisco is a large company with more than sixty thousand people and multiple product divisions. We need to make sure that our alliance communications team is plugged in to the corporate public relations process and that the entire PR team is sensitive to announcements that could affect our strategic relationships. We have also solidified communication with our M&A team so we can provide those team members with input and potential partner reaction when Cisco is involved in acquisitions that might rock the boat with them. While this requires ironclad confidentiality, it frees us up to do the necessary planning to properly position any announcement in the context of our alliance relationship.

Second, it's critical for you to establish a concise communication plan identifying the message you want to convey, how many people will be involved in the process and to whom they will communicate, along with precise timing on how the communications will roll out. This is important because you often have a tight window in which these announcements are made, and you don't want it all going public before you have a chance to brief your partners. Surprising your partners creates the worst of all worlds.

This communication plan can be as simple as the alliance director calling his or her counterpart or can include multiple calls and involvement from multiple managers; it could even be a CEO-to-CEO call in critical situations.

When Cisco bought Navini in 2007, the acquisition instantly positioned us in a segment of the WiMax market, potentially going up against Nokia Siemens Networks (NSN), an important partner. As the deal was being finalized, we developed a business risk paper to understand the deal's impact on the competitive landscape. Then we convened the alliance team and crafted a messaging framework to explain how the deal would affect all partners with special notification to first-line partners like NSN.

We start the process by putting ourselves in our partner's shoes. We explore what the alliance partner would need to communicate this news effectively to its constituencies. When possible, we provide our partner with a comprehensive information package with all the key details and information. This can save it critical time in getting the word out and ensuring that people across its organizations are not surprised and/or wind up misinterpreting the announcement; of course, it's still up to the alliance partner itself whether and how it uses the data. Amazingly, I rarely see other companies go the extra mile and provide this level of communication to their partners, but I believe it's a critical piece of the process of building—and maintaining—trust. It's where the art of the alliance comes into play.

Communication is also critical on the flip side, when a partner makes a potentially negative announcement. For instance, the company might be partnering with one of our rivals or entering a space that could be a competitive threat to us. In these cases, we need to communicate the announcement as quickly as possible, with accurate positioning, to relevant executives and stakeholders in the relationship; we need to properly position the announcement's impact and our response. Expect headaches and problems if your alliance counterparts lack this type of mechanism. At the least, it will make it harder for your team to respond rapidly and appropriately and to get ahead of the curve.

Preempting Future Areas of Conflict

One thing you never want to do is to invite a partner to come in to explore a new opportunity with you when you know your own company is already working on a strategy to pursue that opportunity directly—or has decided to work with a competitor of your alliance partner. You risk destroying trust in the relationship and delivering a nonrecoverable hit. There are two techniques we employ at Cisco to avoid this situation. First, if we clearly have our own strategy, we often refuse to even engage in a discussion; that way, we can't be perceived as milking the partner for information. If we believe our company's strategy is still in flux, we will meet for discussions but use very restrictive nondisclosure agreements to limit the dissemination of our alliance partner's information. We'll also go to extra lengths to explain why. Second, if we've already decided to pursue a business with another partner, we make it very clear to the preexisting partner that it is likely to have significant competition in this market space. We would rather walk away from the discussion rather than risk damaging our alliance.

It all comes down to a simple principle: you have to be accountable to your partners for relationships to endure. If you're honest and forthright, they'll often respect that. Many companies talk about it, but few go beyond lip service; actions are all that count. Being honest, direct, and accountable has helped keep the trust intact during numerous difficult situations in which we're both competing with and cooperating with our alliance partners.

Of course, conflicts can't always be successfully managed. This comes with the territory. And just as you need a plan to manage the alliance and the relationships, you'll also need a plan for leaving the relationship in time while also keeping the door open for future engagement. Retirement of an alliance is the last option. But if you must exit a partnership, approach it as another phase of managing relationships, planning and working through the right process diligently. As part of our strategic alliance life cycle (see figure 1), we include steps for determining an exit strategy, making plans and timelines, and crafting unified messaging around the decision. These include:

- Have a thorough understanding of key elements that have changed since the alliance was formed.

- Map and document the changes—more competitive products, a competitive market positioning/strategy, mergers and acquisitions, consolidations in the market, and so on.

- Propose alternative scenarios for the alliance— transition the alliance to a more tactical relationship, switch the alliance to another department, move to a regional partnership, or retire the alliance.

- Create a scenario document including pros and cons, as well as a recommendation, and then present it to senior and executive staff.

- Once your senior managers agree on a recommended course of action, create retirement documentation, and communicate to the partner and sales organizations.

Through the alliances of ours that have ended, we have learned to never burn bridges—you may be teaming up later. People have long memories of soured relationships, and these ghosts could come back to haunt you.

In many cases, it boils down to common sense. When one of our big partners allied with a competitor on the East Coast for a big government job, I got hit with several e-mail missiles: "How could these guys do this? We should exit the alliance."

My attitude was, take a deep breath and look at the big picture. The alliance is worth a lot to us. Do we really want to sacrifice it because of one rival deal? The internal critics finally relented and we moved on. That alliance is now worth hundreds of millions of dollars a year.

When it comes to relationships, you have to be reasonable. Every day of every week, one of your partners is likely doing something you don't like—you have to look past it and keep your eye on the endgame. Using common sense and reason, you can leverage relationships to steer you through the toughest challenges and help keep even the most fragile alliances rolling along more smoothly.

In the next section, I'll show you how to address the more complex aspects of alliance management.

Managing Complexity

Strategic alliances are anything but simple. If you're like many business leaders, you need to manage an array of alliances. Add them up, and it can start to look like a game of three-dimensional chess: every move affects every other piece, and at any one time, your opponents can be moving three or more pieces simultaneously!

Alliance management at the senior level is all about thinking strategically *and* creatively. Beyond the process and pieces you have on the board, how you manage these complexities determines success. We've seen the importance of developing the right framework, people, and relationships. Now we'll look at the art of the alliance from a higher management perspective, focusing on some of the more complex elements of managing within and across alliance portfolios. These include intellectual property management, portfolio management, the cooperative-competitive dynamic, globalization, and metrics.

Understanding and Managing Intellectual Property

We hear the term *intellectual property* (IP) a lot these days to describe such assets as software, music, technology, logos, and the like. The word *property* implies that the owner of the asset has certain exclusive rights to it (just as owning a piece of real estate means you can exclude others from trespassing), while the word *intellectual* means that the asset isn't tangible—it's something that has value even when carried around in someone's head.

The simplest way to protect intellectual property is to keep it a secret. This is essentially how the formula for Coke and the source code for Windows are protected. If Coca-Cola or Microsoft have a business need to disclose their crown jewels, they do so under highly restrictive confidentiality agreements. If there were a breach of security and those secrets fell into unauthorized hands, trade secret law would provide protection and remedies—including criminal prosecution.

But in many cases, it's impossible to exploit the value of an IP asset without disclosing it publicly. You can't market the Post-it note, for example, without revealing the inventive idea behind it. And by making the secret accessible to millions, you risk turning it into a low-value commodity. This is especially true of digital assets, where the marginal cost of production is virtually zero.

Intellectual property laws are designed to counteract this effect. To reward inventive ideas or unique ways of expressing them, these laws essentially give owners a monopoly on an innovation. Copyright law, for example, protects works of authorship—writings, music, software code, blueprints. The owner of the copyright can prohibit others from copying, distributing, and modifying the work—or alternatively (and more likely), charge a license fee for the privilege.

Patent law rewards novel and useful ideas—new drugs, industrial processes, engineered materials, and in the United States, business methods. Patent laws give an inventor the right to control the use, manufacture, and sale of the invention for a limited period of time (in the United States, about twenty years). In exchange, the inventor has to completely disclose all the details of the invention so that others can build on the discovery.

Another type of intellectual property is trademarks, which guide the public in making purchasing decisions by indicating the source of goods and services. Think of how much value and goodwill are tied up in words like *apple* (when used in conjunction with computers and media devices), *gap* (when used with clothing), *post* (when used with breakfast cereal), and so on. Those words represent investments of millions (sometimes even billions) of dollars to promote public awareness of—and confidence in—the companies that stand behind them.

So when we talk about intellectual property, we are really talking about a number of distinct concepts that are protected under many different legal regimes.

Every company has a different strategy and priorities for building and protecting its IP assets. For example, some companies view their patent portfolio as a profit center—a source of licensing revenues—while others use their patents defensively, to protect their core business from litigation claims by competitors. When you build a strategic alliance, you need to take those differences into account.

Before coming to the table to discuss a strategic alliance, you and your team should first identify what your company and the potential partner are contributing in the form of IP, how it will be enhanced, and whether new IP will be created. You also need to strategize on how to protect and manage IP. Make sure your team works with the affected business units so that they clearly understand the technology, the underlying business strategy, and the potential competitive risks. Then work with your legal team to develop a plan to manage the risks and anticipate the IP issues that will arise.

Here are some examples of IP issues that crop up in alliances:

- **Jointly developed technology:** For technology-oriented alliances, you need to consider the possibility that you and your partner will be creating valuable IP together and to agree in advance on who's going to own it and how the companies will exploit and protect it. Will one company be allowed to exploit the IP independently from the other? If so, will the exploiting company be required to pay royalties to or share profits with the partner? These are difficult and tricky issues that will require much discussion and strategizing.

- **Solutions:** Where's the IP? In many strategic alliances, the partners will contribute their individual IP and jointly architect it in a way that solves a particular customer problem. A solution may consist, for example, of software provided by one partner with a business process performed (and owned) by the other. The question then arises whether there is IP in the solution that's distinct from the IP in each individual component. If there is, you will need to agree on how it will be owned, exploited, and managed.

- **Residuals:** One of the most contentious issues in negotiating the confidentiality terms of an alliance agreement is the treatment of residuals—that is, general knowledge, know-how, and skills that each partner's employees will gain by being exposed to the other partner's confidential information. If the agreement does not have a residuals clause, it may be necessary to firewall those employees from working on similar projects outside the scope of the alliance. Because this creates an administrative and financial burden—and restricts the affected employees' career options—it is strongly recommended that a residuals clause be included in your alliance agreement.

- **Branding:** Strategic alliances often present powerful opportunities for branding synergies. When Cisco allied with Fujitsu to develop routers for the Japan market, the decision was made to cobrand the product. This allowed the companies to leverage Cisco's global reputation for switches and routers with Fujitsu's local reputation for IT equipment and solutions. But before deciding on a branding strategy, you need to do the due diligence. Make sure you know the value of the brand you bring to the table, as well as your partner's. Understand how your respective brands play in the markets that the alliance is intended to address. Cobranding is only one option; in some cases, it may make sense to go with one partner's brand or to come up with a new brand altogether. You also need to evaluate the risks to your brand if the alliance fails and manage them accordingly. Discuss these issues with your company's marketing and branding groups—as well as your trademark counsel—and make sure you have their buy-in.

Managing IP is a challenge that continues through the life of any relationship. Once you've worked out all the IP issues and reached agreement with your partner, you'll also need to brief your team on the continuing risks and obligations. Make sure everyone understands the rules of engagement, what he or she needs to do to protect the company's IP assets, and how to spot (and escalate) red flags.

You'll also need to work closely with your finance and risk-management teams because Sarbanes-Oxley regulations—as well as other countries' laws—may require them to audit IP assets and report any contingencies and changes in value.

Portfolio Management

Most companies do one-off alliances and wonder why their strategy fails. At Cisco, we take a portfolio approach. We start by making sure we understand our business objectives in the technology space where we are considering a build-buy-partner strategy. We then lay out the scope and number of relationships we need to achieve our business objectives. Refining our business goals almost always starts with two questions:

- How do we achieve our desired *global* market position? Markets around the world are being knit together more quickly than ever before. Local or regional barriers to entry are under enormous pressure as markets move from rapid growth to maturity. And the cycle has been compressed dramatically.

- Which pieces of the value chain are central to sustaining our long-term profitability in a market? Note that this answer can vary significantly based on the business model and industry in which your company operates. Options can involve:

  - Building or acquiring your own products or services in parts of the value chain you believe are core

- ○ Investing in companies that are important to the value chain with complementary products
- ○ Allying with companies that help you complete the value chain

Your choice of partner may vary significantly depending on the answers to this question, so you need to think through it very carefully.

Viewing this from a higher level, we believe four factors drive overall profitability across most industries: market timing/entry, market share, capital/investment intensity, and long-term sustainable cost position across the value chain. When we look at the combination of our objectives and the inherent risk in our industry, we have found very few sectors where a single class of partners (such as technology, go-to-market, or enabling technology), or even a single partner within a group, enables us to address our key concerns. Our approach has been to generally follow a multipronged approach, with different time horizons and priorities across our partner portfolio.

Aligning with Multiple Companies in Your Portfolio

Once you've analyzed your objectives and your specific market, you'll want to consider a few approaches to developing a robust portfolio of alliances: depending on your business goals and strategy, you may use any one of these three approaches:

- **Partnering with market leaders:** When Cisco entered the storage-switching market, we realized that our ability to build a market-leading position at either the high or low end would be impossible with just one partner. The leading storage manufacturers (EMC, IBM, HP, and Hitachi) heavily influenced the route to market because they drove the switching vendors' ability to demonstrate product interoperability and supportability. Relationships with more than one player were important, but working with the market leaders was critical.

- **Partnering with market challengers/disruptors:** Entering the fast-growing cellular market required us to position our IP routing and switching technology as an important enabler for the evolution of radio access networks. With that positioning in mind, we worked with a market challenger, Motorola, that had more to gain from disrupting the existing players through its innovation. Working with Motorola, we built solutions that enabled higher reliability at lower costs and created an infrastructure that would better adapt to the rising tide of data traffic.

Partnering with market challengers or disruptors requires you to take risks. These risks can be offset by enormous benefits. First, it gives you invaluable lead time to develop integrated offerings that can differentiate you from everyone else. Disruptors benefit as the market changes quickly—that is, if their entry has a real impact in terms of incremental market share and speed, it will generate a change in the battlefield and the nature of how the battle is fought (such as an alteration of the value chain). Second, this early momentum will often pressure the existing players to take a hard look at the partnering option, particularly if you successfully redefine a market's business or technology model—and are able to sustain the needed investment.

- **Partnering with both:** Creating vertical solutions requires a different partnering model for each segment. In some cases, partnering with market leaders is required. In others, working with disruptors is much more important: one example is when you know the leaders will

> resist and defend a value chain that is re-
> aligning due to technology or market forces.

The widespread destruction following Hurricanes Rita and Katrina accelerated a philosophical shift in the alliance strategy at Habitat for Humanity. Faced with more than five hundred thousand families with destroyed or severely damaged homes in Texas, Louisiana, Mississippi, and Alabama, Habitat knew its own resources would never be enough to meet the demand.

Habitat already had built a strong circle of alliance partners around its core competence of providing affordable homes for purchase by families in need. Members of the management team had long recognized that they needed financial institutions, social service agencies, churches, government organizations, schools, civic groups, corporations, and others to accomplish their mission.

Where Habitat once found itself as the controlling service organization at the hub of a wheel of alliances who all shared a common interest, it now considers itself one of the many spokes. Habitat's role is now seen by its management team as that of a housing "catalyst" to spark awareness about affordable housing issues and generate coordinated, effective action with the elimination of poverty as the common goal. "Leaders from throughout the global Habitat movement realized that the scope of the housing problem—and poverty itself—is so vast that Habitat can't possibly make the necessary impact on its own," said Marty Kooistra, the twenty-year veteran who leads Habitat's alliances program. "Through our alliance network, we serve as the integrative thinkers . . . figuring out how all of our partners can succeed."

Spreading Your Alliance Bets

Sometimes you need to spread your bets to deal with uncertainty. You need to consider five criteria when you evaluate the breadth of an alliance portfolio within a market space:

- **Market share:** What is your desired/required market share over a three- to five-year period in this market? Based on your answers, the size, number, and type of partners may vary significantly.

- **Market segmentation:** If you decide you need multiple partnerships, you can attempt to further segment the market and position each relationship slightly differently. Some potential segmentation variables would include geography, vertical industries, or location in the value chain.

- **Competitive overlap:** Ask yourself two critical questions: What is the probability of you or your partner competing in the space in which you are currently collaborating? What pressures in other market segments where you compete could force either company to exit the relationship at the corporate level?

- **Potential acquisition strategy:** You must manage the probability that one of your competitors could acquire your partner and therefore disrupt your market strategy. There are mechanisms you can employ to mitigate that risk, such as first right of refusal or joint venture / technology buyout clauses.

- **Ability to execute:** Your market strategy could fail as a result of either your own company's or the partner's inability to succeed in the relationship.

Managing a portfolio of alliances within a market or technology space is a complex task. If you're managing a portfolio of relationships that span business sectors, the complexity grows exponentially. The problem is that strategic partnering decisions are naturally often made by business or alliance leaders with knowledge in the relevant market. But because of their narrow focus, they may be completely unaware of any impact their decisions might have on the broader cross-company relationships.

Part of your role is to head off these potential conflicts. That means creating scenarios for the evolution of a broad portfolio and making sure that executives across the various divisions understand the broader implications and trade-offs to consider. Let's discuss ways that can be done.

Creating a Shared Framework and Portfolio Model

Crafting a strategy for each market sector is a foundational building block of your alliance strategy. You may have multiple alliance components within a sector and then multiple sectors, depending on the size of your company and nature of your markets. By piecing together these elements, you can begin to develop an overall picture of the value of an individual partner's relationship to your company and how this compares to other players in your portfolio.

It helps to outline the long-term value of relationships by sector and then to scan across all the sectors and determine the importance and value of each partnership to your company, using tools such as financial projections and market coverage maps.

Standard portfolio management techniques can help as you try to position for various future scenarios and stay on top of market and competitive trends. You have to identify the variables you believe could have the most significant impact on your portfolio of alliances. The most important variables we monitor at Cisco are market and business model disruptions, adjacency moves, significant changes in customer buying behavior, and "blue oceans" of uncontested market space ripe for growth. While there may be many variables that drive changes to your company overall, there are usually relatively few that will have a significant impact on your portfolio balance and strategy. The trick is to identify these variables and then build plans to deal with them.

For example, we saw consolidation coming to the major players in the telecommunications equipment supplier market due to industry overcapacity, a fundamental technology change, and our own growth aspirations. We had to make quick adjustments that included tilting our alliance strategy toward more regional players and away from multiple global players that posed potential product overlaps that would be difficult to manage, and more toward more IT services firms that did not have a significant product portfolio in the segments we were pursuing.

Building Relevant Portfolio Scenarios

Once you have identified the variables that you will track to alter your portfolio, your alliance management team should define future scenarios. You need to identify both the opportunities and threats associated with moves you could make or moves that others in the industry could make. Your alliance management team needs to work closely with relevant business heads and cross-functional teams to create simple names for these scenarios that reflect the scenarios' underlying nature. Then they need to outline the potential impact on your alliance strategy.

It is important that you quantify the impact of these scenarios on your overall alliance strategy. What would be the increased costs to your company? Lost product sales? Or, in the worst case, what if you had to exit from selected markets? Because the technology industry changes so quickly, we plan scenarios in three- to five-year time horizons rather than the common five- to ten-year horizons.

Look for trigger points—those events that could signal a material change in the environment and could impact one of the swing variables you discovered earlier. You can capture this information at the alliance level through a traditional SWOT (strength, weakness, opportunity, threat) analysis or by carefully watching the moves your partners make with competitors through a competitive landscape map. Alliance leaders must work closely with their business development colleagues to keep abreast of acquisition strategies or significant moves that could affect one or more alliances.

Once you've laid out the baseline case for a future scenario and several plausible alternatives, it's important to discuss this with the key players on the senior management team. You need to discuss specific recommendations that better leverage the alliance portfolio and mitigate potential risk. Schedule periodic reviews with relevant cross-functional or cross-divisional senior management teams. And consider establishing an alliance board with representatives spanning both market sectors and functions within your company. You want to engage them as much as possible so they will participate in evolving and communicating your strategy.

I believe that developing and actively managing an alliance portfolio is one of the best ways to deliver true value to your company. The portfolio approach provides you substantial market leverage over your competition while mitigating your overall risk. But that's not enough. You need to take a close look at the nature of competition itself and how that fits within your overall strategy.

The Cooperative-Competitive Dynamic

In many industries, customers are struggling with the convergence and complexity of technologies. They are overwhelmed with the speed, complexity, and rate of change. They want simplicity and choice. However, no one company has the ability to offer every product and service across all components of the value chain. Partnering with rivals helps companies fill in the gaps.

Those players who work to address the issues of complexity can experience significant business value. These companies can integrate their products and services to provide simple answers to solve real customer problems.

Of course, you face considerable risk in partnering with a competitor. You could open your doors to a company that could hurt you in your own market over time, gain competitive advantages, or acquire unique knowledge or skills that it could not have obtained otherwise. You could also send a confusing message to your customers and sales organizations, which could either slow down purchasing or create credibility problems for your teams. Finally, you run the risk of confusing other partners; they may be baffled by your allying with another company that they compete against in some markets.

So then, why work with competitors? It makes sense to collaborate with competitors when partnering accomplishes one of the following four goals:

- **Creates additional customer choice and confidence:** In the technology market, the availability of interoperable solutions from multiple vendors can accelerate overall market growth or create a larger market opportunity that benefits many companies. The larger market opportunity could result from investments being moved from other portions of the customer's budget or other areas of the company value chain, which would either increase top-line growth or reduce operating expenses. One example is collaboration around industry standards or open interfaces. In 2007, even though Cisco indicated we would be competing with Microsoft in unified communications, we announced an extension to our alliance in other areas and an interoperability road map with Microsoft in the unified communications space. Both of us benefited from market changes in the unified communications space, and product interoperability was key to our customers' confidence in moving forward on their decisions even though our approaches differed.

Blue Cross and Blue Shield of Florida (BCBSF) linked up in 2001 with a competitor (Humana, Inc.) and another regional Blue plan in 2006 to create a joint venture. Alliances let BCBSF contain costs and reach the scale it needed to compete with national players while providing access to new markets, explains Bridget Booth, principal of BCBSF's alliance program. "Teaming up with a competitor may sound like flawed logic on the surface. Yet for us, it was the right answer for lowering health costs and improving service."

The joint venture created an innovative Internet-based solution that streamlines administrative workflow and improves communication between physicians, hospitals, customers, and pharmacies. The results: lower health costs, improved efficiencies, and more timely service to customers, physicians, and hospitals.

- **Represents a clearly delineated and contained competitive space:** In some cases, competitive activity is simply dwarfed by the advantages that can come from collaborating. In 2007, IBM purchased a company that overlaps with Cisco's security products. Our collaboration with IBM spans many technologies beyond security. Although we have become more competitive, the security space will probably affect less than 10 percent of the relationship. We both believe it can be managed.

- **Builds competitive advantage for both players:** The partnership can help both companies better compete against other competitive offerings in the same market or against approaches using different business models, even though the companies still compete head-to-head. Both companies must feel they can gain more market share than they could lose to each other.

- **Influences a partner's strategy:** This goal is helpful when you know you can use collaborative activities to create more mutual value than mutual destruction and ultimately move the competition in a favorable direction. The idea is to create mutual value and grow the overall pie by providing more opportunity that outweighs the competitive overlap. It does not mean you stop competing; it means you focus your collective efforts on the customer and growing the market more than on a strategy of mutual self-destruction for a smaller pie.

Managing a competitive relationship is, by its nature, time consuming and difficult. That's why you need to start with the end in mind: collaborating and competing are easiest when the companies' product offerings are segmented by market sector, sales channels, or by product/technology. Today Cisco competes directly with many of our partners in selected market spaces. We compete with HP's ProCurve networking group but collaborate with HP in unified communications. For many years we collaborated extensively with Motorola to develop joint solutions for cellular operators while we competed head-on in the cable market. Areas in which you collaborate with a partner should have offerings and route-to-market models that are clearly differentiated from the areas in which you two compete.

Partners need to be clear with each other, with customers, and with their own employees about when and where they are competing and collaborating. If not, distrust and confusion will outweigh the benefits. This has to be simple and understandable to everyone. You also need to make sure any possible collaboration undergoes careful review by antitrust lawyers and adheres to the laws of countries in which you intend to operate.

Finally, you must have a well-established set of ground rules to manage information security and intellectual property rights. These might include:

- Setting clear parameters in your agreements that identify the information to be shared and the permitted use of such information. In certain instances, it may be necessary to restrict information to some employees and to set up firewalls to prevent tainting other groups within the company that are developing similar technology independently.

- Having a clear understanding of and agreement on the data-security measures that will be used to protect each party's information.

- Identifying and managing the exchange and development of intellectual property and agreeing in advance on each party's rights to jointly developed technology. It is also important to have processes for rapidly escalating and resolving potential conflicts.

- Setting up training and procedures to protect your partner's confidential information and watching for actions by your partner that may signal an improper use of your own information. This is a significant risk when your partner is also a competitor. Although intentional misuse of confidential information is rare in the alliance world, poor training and sloppy procedures raise the likelihood that someone may give in to temptation and share a partner's information with a colleague who doesn't really have a "need to know."

Alliance teams must understand how to clearly delineate between competitive and collaborative activities and the information required to support each. You don't want the wrong information flowing from one partner to another. The phrase "loose lips sink ships" applies here. Then there's the case where the risks of continued collaboration outweigh the benefits of collaboration. If things go wrong, you need a clear set of guidelines and criteria for terminating the relationship.

Globalization: Collaboration Without Borders

As Thomas Friedman so presciently wrote in his best-selling book *The World Is Flat*, the competitive playing field between developed and developing countries has been leveled in this latest era of globalization. Multiple factors are driving this "flattening," including an increasingly educated labor pool, rapid GDP growth in emerging economies, and technologies that allow services and collaboration around these services to be delivered from anywhere in the world. Value chains are being reconfigured across multiple industries, from manufacturing and IT to medical services and even high-end R&D. Companies that aren't viewing their markets and their supply and value chains through a global lens may be seeing only half the picture.

And those companies are in for a rude surprise. Today any company can create a competitive advantage if it focuses its resources on areas where it can create sustainable value by using new global networks to deliver goods and services. This means an alliances strategy must plan for the evolution of the company's partner portfolio through two global filters:

- **Access to and knowledge of future high-growth markets:** Access to high-growth markets like India, China, and other emerging economies may require working closely with players that have significant political and economic presence in those geographies—and deep knowledge of the local business environment. Failing to participate in the fast-growing markets of these countries may put your company at a significant competitive disadvantage in several years. You need to ask yourself today where these markets fit in your business plans. Then you can figure out which partnerships you will need to stay ahead of the curve in these markets.

Growth opportunities are just the beginning. You have to look at other factors, too. The markets for your products and services in developing geographies are often being driven by the huge bottom of the pyramid. This requires you to implement radically lower cost structures to offer products at prices that people in developing countries can afford. This approach forces companies to reassemble value chains to meet these needs at dramatically lower costs. Working with companies focusing on these market segments and building "just good enough" capabilities at dramatically lower price points is good business—and a potential predictor of things to come. Indeed, these models may prove to be major disruptive forces around the globe as they emerge.

- **New business models from anywhere:** You have to be quick on your feet in the new global market. Almost anywhere you operate, you could face companies with vastly different business models moving to drastically alter the landscape where you compete or collaborate.

This could help you create a significant opportunity—or pose a strategic threat if you fail to take advantage, leaving the opportunity open to others. We at Cisco have seen this scenario replayed many times in the information technology industry:

○ Google, based in the United States, is using Internet and systems technology to disrupt the advertising industry while using its advertising revenues to upset segments of the technology industry.

○ Indian-based IT firms like Wipro and Infosys have created global services businesses using a combination of highly skilled but low-cost labor and innovative business processes that can deliver value remotely.

○ China-based Huawei has used a combination of low-cost engineering resources and unique home market conditions to create a significant presence in the global telecom industry.

○ Software-as-a-service models are emerging to address consumer markets, small- to medium-business markets, and enterprise markets.

Examples are prevalent across multiple industries with players emerging from virtually everywhere.

Don't assume these disruptive business models are confined to the technology industry. These conditions can just as easily be developing in your business; if so, you must begin to adapt your alliance investment model to the new global realities. This does not mean you fly people in twice a year to visit companies in other countries. It means that you think *every day* about building relationships with companies that can help you take advantage of the new opportunities and risks that a "flattened" world create. Six basic steps can lead you along this path:

- Understand your value chain, and analyze the impact that innovative models from companies in high-growth emerging economies could have on your business.

- Build your knowledge of these companies' capabilities. This can start with secondary research but should progress to on-the-ground investigations, with a team focused entirely on evaluating your alliance options in these emerging markets.

- Using the lead-follow model we highlighted at the end of section 3, position your alliance resources close to your partners' resources to gain a better understanding of the cultural challenges, as well as the opportunities that relationships with these companies could provide. You need to build not only targeted business plans for these markets, but also knowledge and *trust*. At Cisco, we decided several years ago that we needed to create one globally integrated team for emerging market alliances to ensure one consistent model and the sharing of best practices for managing these complex relationships. We are building our own alliances hub in India to deal both with U.S. companies building major delivery centers there and with India-based IT services companies.

- Based on your criteria, identify an initial partner and a target market. Then establish a working relationship and business model with the partner who meets your criteria. If you can, start small to gain knowledge of both the company and the new culture in which you will be working. Keeping things under the radar is a good idea as you build these new types of relationships. You and your partner both need space to learn as you move forward.

- When working with companies in some foreign markets, strive to understand their company's agenda as well as their national agenda. In the IT industry, companies operating in China and India are often quite committed to helping advance their government's agendas as well as their own. You need to be aware of this when discussing the goals for the relationship.

- Develop a strategy using collaboration tools to help you work more effectively with geographically dispersed companies. Build extranets, wikis, webinars, and video conferencing technologies that enable partners to share information and work together virtually. Translate the material on some of your sites into the language of the local partner, as Cisco did with Fujitsu in Japan. We are continuing to build a video-conferencing network of meeting rooms around the globe at our sites and soon will be expanding this network to include sites with our partners. These types of tools are becoming an essential part of global alliance management and can create a new model for effective collaboration across time zones and geographies.

Bottom line: you're selling your organization short if you fail to think globally and build the capability to operate an alliance from whatever corner of the world makes sense for your company. You always have options; just make sure your alliance model enables you to take advantage of the best ones available.

Metrics: Measuring Your Overall Alliance Return

At the beginning of the book, I talked about the reasons to invest in alliances compared with the many other alternatives you have as a CEO. So how do you make this call? The impact of strategic alliances can best be summarized by one word—*leverage*. Alliances can help you leverage your:

- **Financial performance:** This metric is the easiest to track and generally can be quantified according to incremental top-line revenue impact, saved or reduced investment, or actual ROI over multiple years based on incremental cash flows after investment.

- **Time to market:** This can be harder to quantify but can be measured based on incremental market share over multiple years in terms of customer acquisition.

- **Market access:** Depending on the type of market access that is being measured, this metric could range from dramatically reducing entry costs to serve a particular market, access to key accounts, or the incremental revenue and long-term sustainable market share that could be enabled by being first.

- **Competitive market position:** Improved market share or long-term sustainability from working with an industry leader can dramatically improve your profitability and ability to address and sustain multiple market opportunities.

- **Core competencies and people:** It's also hard to quantify the effect of forcing your company's employees to address other areas of the value chain to address a market opportunity. The easiest way is to look at the opportunity cost of losing this resource given your present operating model. Currently at Cisco, our revenue per employee is around $600,000 per year. This means if we are forced to invest significant human resources in new areas of the value chain for which we are not well suited, we are probably walking away from opportunities that could generate that level of return with possibly much lower risk.

In any alliance organization, you must have a metrics framework that you can apply consistently across all your alliances. At Cisco, we look at alliances using two types of frameworks. One is the annual review of the operating dashboard, which measures an alliance's performance against the key mutually agreed-on business initiatives.

Metrics in these dashboards include:

- Incremental revenue

- Incremental market share in comparison with our competitors

- New customer acquisition/account penetration

- Offset operating expenses

- Net incremental value of new business development activities

- New joint standards that accelerate our market and market positions

- Solutions performance

- Mutual satisfaction/partnership health

- Customer satisfaction with combined offerings

- Return on joint marketing efforts

The second framework is one based on long-term ROI over multiple years. We track long-term financial performance, assessing the cash flow generated by each partnership over and above the investment we are making across the company. And you should track by partnership the incremental investment you are making, whether it is in channel development, joint R&D, joint marketing, alliance team management, or something else. Then compare that with the business you are generating with the partnership.

At Cisco, we try to examine the relationship from both parties' perspectives, with a 360-degree view of the total return to both companies across the entire relationship, by looking at sell with, sell to, sell through, and other nonmonetary variables.

By doing this, Cisco has been able to generate an alliance-specific return and an overall portfolio return that enables us to compare returns to alternative potential investments. On average, we have seen that the payback on our up-front alliance investment tends to be around eighteen months. At that point, the alliance is either gaining momentum because the right foundation has been put in place, or we are clearly having problems. If we are moving in the right direction at this point, the alliance is likely to generate increasing levels of profitability over its life cycle. We know that because most of the investment—and risk—typically occurs during the early phase.

At the end of the day, as a senior executive, you can expect the alliance team to provide you some level of understanding about how the investment of resources stacks up against everything else on your plate. But it's up to *you* to provide team members the resources to develop the tools and information systems needed to make sure they can actually deliver the *information* you need to measure relative performance of this investment against others.

Nothing is simple in this 3-D alliance chess game. It requires a range of strategies to manage alliances in an increasingly complex world, where little is predictable and change is constant. Portfolios, partnering with competitors, a global approach, and integrated metrics are all part of your alliance toolkit. Without these, you'll struggle to bring your company to the next level of alliance management. But with them, you can leap ahead and surpass your goals, advancing and creating new opportunities for your company. It's all about thinking strategically and creatively. It's all about thinking strategically and creatively. It's all about the art of the alliance.

Bringing It Together

The world continues to change quickly, with information and knowledge becoming more transparent and communicated almost instantaneously. Markets are becoming global overnight, and customers are continuing to demand more creative and simpler solutions. In this environment, strategic alliances can and should be an essential part of your business strategy, helping create a competitive playing field that is tipped in your favor. Remember, it's all about leverage!

Alliances, done right, can generate significant and sustainable business value compared to other investment priorities by:

- Accelerating your market access in adjacent or new market spaces and creating new top-line revenue growth

- Enabling you to focus on those places in your value chain that leverage your core competencies and therefore reduce your costs and risks in attaining this top-line revenue growth

- Providing you a way to balance business risk, create competitive advantage, and help move the market by leveraging an integrated portfolio strategy model

- Helping you create sustainable and differentiated value

Building a successful alliance strategy, however, will require a new mind-set that may be foreign to many executives. Alliances are art *and* science, people *and* process. It's a "both/and" way of thinking rather than an "either/or." Alliances only make sense if you do them right. That means linking them to your business strategy, building a repeatable and sustainable framework, staffing them with the right people, and providing those people with the necessary resources to think and act globally.

Creating strategic alliances is not for those companies that manage their business on a quarter-to-quarter basis, that are unwilling to take risk, and that do not make the investment required to do it well. If you find yourself in one of those categories, don't waste your time trying to build sustainable alliances.

The only sustainable item you will have is a stream of press clippings announcing new partnerships and the constant embarrassment that follows when you are asked for the alliance results. Building strategic alliances is all about re-aligning the playing field for true sustainable advantage. Doing that requires the same preparation, thought process, and dedication as any other significant strategy decision.

If you are willing to make the necessary commitment as the leader of your organization to build this into your business strategy and invest in everything required to do it well, then get moving. In a globally linked business world with shortening life cycles and flattening value chains, building alliances capabilities will give you the chance to tilt the competitive playing field in your favor and significantly enhance your company's or organization's chance for long-term success.

Appendix

FIGURE 2

Job responsibilities for a Cisco alliance manager

Core	Advanced	Most senior
• Manage estab-lished alliance initiatives	• Build and nurture alliance relationships to ensure alignment	• Establish and foster executive relationships and secure buy-in
• Research new alliance initiatives and opportunities	• Drive new alliance initiatives and opportunities	• Define alliance framework and value proposition; create breakthrough opportunities
• Provide tactical advice to alliance partners	• Act as a strategic adviser to alliance partners and business units	• Contribute to portfolio strategy
• Support field en-gagement activities	• Design and develop solutions	• Lead and manage partner initiatives
• Participate in virtual teams	• Manage field engagement	• Identify new strate-gies and incentives for field engage-ment and business success
• Implement solutions	• Create and manage governance for projects and initiatives owned	• Create and provide leadership in virtual teams
• Apply governance standards	• Create and manage governance struc-ture for alliances	• Create and pursue new market solutions
• Contribute to fiscal-year plan-ning activities	• Contribute to and/or lead alliance fiscal-year planning	• Create and manage governance struc-ture for alliances
	• Oversee business plan development and presentation	• Contribute to and/or lead alliance fiscal-year planning

FIGURE 3

Deliverables for a Cisco alliance manager

Core	Advanced	Most senior
• Project and program plans	• Project and program plans with expanded scope	• Everything in two left-hand columns with greater scope and ownership, adding:
• Project execution/delivery	• Solution definition	• Fiscal-year business plan contribution or ownership if manager of an alliance
• Project communication to stakeholders	• Feedback about partner's activities, technology trends, and response plans	• Reporting (quarterly reports, operation reviews, CEO briefings)
• Input to customer presentations	• Alliance and customer presentations	• New-market solutions
• Content input for business cases	• Business case or strategic plan for alliance solutions and initiatives	• Input into alliance portfolio strategy
• Contributions to executive briefing documents	• Executive briefing document and meeting facilitation	• Escalation resolution
• Agreements (non-disclosure, statements of work, letters of intent)	• Agreements (binding, purchase, technology, licensing, collaboration)	• Negotiation of broader agreements
	• Governance framework for solutions and initiatives	• Executive buy-in and sponsorship
	• Joint development program road maps	• Board meeting agenda (briefings and preparation of materials)
		• Alliance governance framework

FIGURE 4

Metrics for a Cisco alliance manager

Core	Most senior
• Attributed revenue	• Executive linkage, pairing, and planning
• Market share for Cisco	• Strategic positioning of new markets
• Value of joint solution wins with customers	• Breadth of alliance portfolio
• Migration of Cisco content to partner solutions	• Quality of business plan
• Quality of alliance relationship (mutual commitment to work through challenges, competitive areas)	• Performance against business plan
• Adoption of technology strategy (Cisco and partner vision alignment)	• Market penetration (geographies and segments)
• Removal of overlaps and competitive threats (taken away from competition)	• Scalability of alliances
• Performance against objectives	• Effectiveness/success of the alliance to partner in creating or entering in a new market
	• Transition or retirement of an alliance or alliance initiative

FIGURE 5

Skills for a Cisco alliance manager

Core

- Analytical thinking
- Building executive relationships
- Business acumen
- Business networking
- Competitor knowledge
- Consulting and partnering
- Cultural adaptability
- Customer knowledge
- Data analysis
- Decision making
- Facilitation
- Industry/vertical knowledge
- Influence
- Interpersonal communication
- Joint value creation
- Learning agility
- Legal and ethical compliance
- Partner/vendor management
- Planning and prioritization
- Presentation and demonstration
- Project management
- Sales process knowledge
- Team effectiveness
- Time and productivity management

Advanced

- Conflict management
- Enterprise perspective
- Goal alignment
- Innovation management
- Negotiation
- Portfolio management
- Risk identification and management
- Routes-to-market strategy and planning
- Strategic business planning

Acknowledgments

I want to thank a number of people and organizations for their contributions in helping to create the material for this book.

First and foremost is the management team at Cisco that has always been extremely supportive of strategic alliances as a key part of our overall company business strategy. They continue to provide us the necessary resources to execute our innovative plans. This group includes John Chambers, Rick Justice, Charlie Giancarlo, Mike Volpi, and Dan Scheinman. I'm also grateful for the ongoing support from all the functional leaders across Cisco whose organizations are such a critical part of the equation that make our alliances successful.

Second is the great alliances team I have had the pleasure to work with over the past several years. They have really been the source for many of the ideas and best practices outlined in this book. They continue to be a source of inspiration to me with their commitment to excellence and their constant drive to find better ways to create and manage these complex entities we call "strategic alliances." A special thanks to my senior management team of Lou Cirillo, Rick Esker, Greg Fox, Simon Hayes, Bob Merry, Greg Prynn, Pascal Turchi, Eric Wenig, my executive administrator Donna Walters, and my extended management team of David Lim and Carmen Cortez. They make my job a pleasure.

Third are our alliance partners who have worked with us to build our relationships into win-win models. We have had the pleasure to work with many of them for several years. Together we have created innovative new ways to deliver value to our customers and shareholders.

Fourth is the team that helped turn our alliances work into the book that's in your hands. The team that pulled the material together and provided invaluable feedback throughout the editing process starts with the folks at Harvard Business Press (Jacque Murphy, Carolyn Monaco, Jennifer Waring, and many others). It continues with my internal team here at Cisco with Brad Whitworth (communications), Marina Grant (best practices), Mark Douglas (metrics), and Elaine Foreman and Alan Stern (legal), and Mark Ivey who provided the editorial polish.

Acknowledgments

Finally I would like to express my gratitude to my entire family. Thanks to my parents who provided me the opportunity and education to prepare me for the future. And thanks to my wife Lucia and my children Nick and Alexis who have put up with the crazy work hours and travel schedules that have been a necessary part of my strategic alliances role here at Cisco (and before!). I could not ask for a more understanding and supportive family who make my business and personal life a win-win environment.

I also want you to know that profits from the sale of this book will be used by the Cisco Foundation to bring the power of the Internet and communications technology to underserved communities around the world.

—Steve

Notes

1. Kees Cools and Alexander Roos, *The Role of Alliances in Corporate Strategy* (Boston, MA: Boston Consulting Group, 2005).

2. Association of Strategic Alliance Professionals, *The Second State of Alliance Management Study 2007* (Needham, MA: Association of Strategic Alliance Professionals, March 2007), 5.

3. Lawrence Owen et al., "The Power of Many" (Armonk, NY: IBM Global Business Services, 2006); David Ernst and Tammy Halevy, "Not by M&A Alone," *McKinsey Quarterly*, no. 1 (2004); John Harbison and Peter Pekar, *Smart Alliances: A Practical Guide to Repeatable Success* (San Francisco: Jossey-Bass, 1998), 56–57.

4. James D. Bamford, Benjamin Gomes-Casseres, and Michael S. Robinson, *Mastering Alliance Strategy: A Comprehensive Guide to Design, Management, and Organization* (San Francisco: Jossey-Bass, 2003), 31.

5. Leila Abboud, "How Eli Lilly's Monster Deal Faced Extinction—but Survived," *Wall Street Journal* (April 27, 2005).

6. Bamford, Gomes-Casseres, and Robinson, *Mastering Alliance Strategy*, 149–162.

7. Joanne Sammer, "Strategic Alliances: How to Manage, How to Measure," *Business Finance* (March 2004).

8. Jim Collins, *Good to Great* (New York: Harper Business, 2001).

9. Association of Strategic Alliance Professionals, *2008 ASAP Salary Survey* (Needham, MA: Association of Strategic Alliance Professionals, 2008).

10. Ibid.

11. Bamford, Gomes-Casseres, and Robinson, *Mastering Alliance Strategy*, 195.

12. Michael J. Marquardt, Steven B. King, and William Ershkine, *International Comparisons: ASTD's Annual Accounting of Worldwide Patterns in Employer-Provided Training* (Alexandria, VA: American Society for Training & Development, 2002).

13. Harbison and Pekar, *Smart Alliances*, 145.

14. Curt Volkmann, "Online Alliance Training and Support at Dow," online paper, American Society for Training & Development, February 2001.

15. Harbison and Pekar, *Smart Alliances*, 145–146.

16. Kenneth Klee, "Lilly's Prescription for Growth," *Corporate Dealmaker*, Summer 2004.

17. Bamford, Gomes-Casseres, and Robinson, *Mastering Alliance Strategy*, 119–120.

18. Abboud, "How Eli Lilly's Monster Deal Faced Extinction—But Survived."

About the Author

Steve Steinhilber is Vice President of Strategic Alliances at Cisco Systems, responsible for driving the development of new strategic alliances and ongoing management of the company's top global alliances, among them Accenture, Hewlett-Packard, IBM, Intel, Microsoft, Motorola, Nokia, and WiPro. During Steinhilber's tenure, Cisco has been recognized by both business and academia for alliance leadership and excellence. The Association of Strategic Alliance Professionals (ASAP) has awarded Cisco its Alliance Excellence Award four of the last six years.

Before joining Cisco, Steinhilber was Vice President of product management and technical support at interWAVE Communications International. He also served as Vice President of the Adaptive division of NET, and has held domestic and international sales and general management positions at Concurrent Computer and at AT&T.

Steinhilber is a member of analyst firm IDC's Alliance Executive Panel. He also serves on Cisco's

Enterprise Business Council and Service Provider Business Council. He has been a featured speaker at the Conference Board, the Management Roundtable, ASAP, and Stanford Speaker's Breakfast, and served as keynote presenter and cochair at the CoDev 2005 conference.

Steinhilber holds a BA from Duke University and an MBA from Harvard Business School.